CW01024374

# BEASTLY MERSEYSIDE

**Ken Pye** FLHU

AMBERLEY

First published 2022

Amberley Publishing
The Hill, Stroud
Gloucestershire, GL5 4EP

www.amberley-books.com



ISBN 978 1 3981 0794 6 (print)
ISBN 978 1 3981 0795 3 (ebook)



British Library Cataloguing in Publication Data.
A catalogue record for this book is available from the British Library.

Typesetting by SJmagic DESIGN SERVICES, India.
Printed in Great Britain.

# Contents

# Introduction

Over the years, in many books that I have published, DVD documentaries and audio CDs that I have produced, and in many hundreds of talks, lectures, and presentations that I have given about the history and heritage of Liverpool and Merseyside, I have always missed out one of the most crucial elements. I talk about the people, the communities, the architecture, and the incidents, but I have never seriously talked about the vital role played by animals in our historical timeline.

We have always needed animals for food and clothing, to labour for us, to supply power and energy, and to transport us and our goods. We have also used them to provide entertainment and sport and, if they were lucky and we loved them, to be our companions. Some special animals guide us when we cannot see or hear, and others have carried messages for us. Sadly, so many have died, and continue to die, because of our exploitation of them. Also, their very existence has been essential to the development, capacity, and nature of humanity. Sadly, and as throughout history, we still do take the world's animals for granted.

This book now shifts the emphasis away from humanity and towards the animal kingdom. It does so by telling of the many roles played in our history and modern lives by all kinds of creatures. In so doing, I hope to awaken in my readers recognition and appreciation of how little mankind would have progressed, and how different our existences would be, without the lives, sacrifices, toil, and love of those other creatures who share our world, the animals.

# 1. In the Beginning

## When Dinosaurs Ruled Merseyside

Animal life (and plant life also, of course) was present on the face of the earth for millions of years before man was even a twinkle in the eye of God; we are a very 'Johnny-come-lately' species. Logic would dictate that by right of prior tenancy alone they have more right to be on the planet than we have, and yet, we have a history of taking them for granted and exploiting them ruthlessly. Fortunately, our intelligence and capacity mean that, at heart, most of us today recognise our responsibility towards animals, and that we care for and love them; Liverpool and Merseyside are a microcosm of this.

The first animal of any significance to leave the seas and walk on the shores of this region left its traces in rocks dug from the ancient quarries at Storeton on the Wirral. These are important historical sites and provided stone for man's local building projects from around 2,000 years ago. The quarries were originally up to 200 feet deep in places but are now disused and overgrown with woodlands. The whole area is now a popular nature reserve.

It was the Roman invaders who first excavated here, in the first century AD, to find stone for their local buildings. The quarries remained in use well into the twentieth century, when a Victorian tramway was still being used to transport stone throughout the area, and to the docks at Bromborough Pool.

The quarries also became an important archaeological site in the nineteenth century. This was when quarrymen began to discover sets of fossilised animal tracks in the slabs of stone they were cutting, and palaeontologists later identified these as belonging to a prehistoric creature called 'Chirotherium'.

Storeton Quarry in the early twentieth century. (Discover Liverpool Library)

Chirotherium footprint. (Discover Liverpool Library)

In the Triassic Period, around 250 million years ago, which was the beginning of the 'Age of the Great Reptiles', what is now Merseyside was prowled by this dinosaur. Its name means 'Hand Beast' because of the five-fingered shape of its fossilised footprints. This great lizard measured about 2½ metres long, stood around 1½ metres tall, and had a slim but muscular body with a long, powerful tail. It may have been amphibious and perhaps a relative of the crocodile, because it had long rows of strong, sharp teeth and was undoubtedly carnivorous. A life-size model of this creature is on display in the World Museum Liverpool.

Slabs with the preserved footprints are also on display in the museum as well as in the Williamson Art Gallery in Birkenhead. Other footprints of the Chirotherium can still also been seen, at certain times, on the shore at Crosby, just to the north of Liverpool, but the best local examples came from Storeton.

What has also been learned is that the Hand Beast was not the only local dinosaur, because we also had 'Rhyncosaurus', which means 'Snouted Lizard'. Examples of this creature's tracks were found in a quarry in Rathbone Street, in Liverpool. It was a herbivore that had a long, hooked beak for grubbing up roots. It also had powerful jaws and strong teeth for tearing down and chewing tough plants.

Rhyncosaurus too was large and stood about 1 metre high and 2 metres long. It was also very heavy to have left such deep and lasting footprints in the mud of prehistoric Merseyside. This animal may have been powerfully built but, unfortunately for the Snouted Lizard, it was the main food supply of Chirotherium!

Chirotherium model in the World Museum Liverpool. (Discover Liverpool Library)

Whilst our local dinosaurs may not have been truly spectacular monsters, like T-Rex or Brachiosaurus, they were certainly formidable enough, and show that animal life of one form or another has been around on Merseyside for a very long time indeed.

## Wild Boars, Bears, Wolves, and the Royal Hunt

As prehistoric and Neolithic man appeared in this part of Britain, and settled into communities and tribes of hunter-gatherers, the relationship between man and all kinds of animal species began to change radically. This was when humanity realised that it had power and capacity enough to overcome and dominate most animals. However, bears survived in Britain until around the seventh century, and wolves until the late seventeenth century, together with wild boars. Even though, up to the early Middle Ages, certain animals tried to eat us when the opportunity provided itself, we also hunted them for food – although we did so for sport too.

Certainly, from the time of the Norman Conquest of England in 1066, the laws put in place by the new ruler, King William the Conqueror (*c.* 1028–87), and his successor monarchs, restricted the right to hunt wild animals, especially deer, to the monarchy and aristocracy only. Indeed, the penalties meted out to the generally starving peasantry for hunting or poaching on royal estates, or those of the landed gentry, ranged from blinding and mutilation (cutting off lips, noses, ears, fingers, hands, or feet) to death by hanging.

From early Celtic times (600 BC to AD 50), and later the Anglo-Saxon period (AD 410 to 1066), many species of animals were being domesticated and bred for meat, milk, eggs, leather, and wool. This remained the case after the Conquest, although such animals and the land they grazed on, though husbanded and farmed by ordinary people, were owned by the aristocracy. Such was the case in and around Liverpool and what would become Merseyside. The Norman kings themselves held territory across the region, or they leased it out to their peers, the Barons and Earls.

At that time and when allowed, hunting was important for food for ordinary people but mostly as sport for the king and the aristocracy. There were royal hunting forests on Wirral: at Simonswood (near Kirkby and West Derby); at Hale's Wood (which became Halewood); and the largest of all, the Toxteth Forest in south Liverpool.

The name of this large and ancient tract of land, covering more than 2,000 acres, was 'Toxteth'. This name was derived from the Celtic name of a local farm that translated as 'Toki's Steading'. This huge forest is mentioned in early records as 'Stochestede', indeed implying a stockaded area to protect livestock.

In 1207, King John (1166–1216) bought the Toxteth forest and district from the Molyneux family, who owned all this part of southern Liverpool at that time. This covered an area from what is now Parliament Street out to Garston, and from modern Smithdown (Esmedune) Road across to the banks of the Mersey. John then stockaded the entire district of Toxteth and created a private hunting forest for himself and his courtiers, and he used this regularly.

The King employed a Master Huntsman and forty-nine Wardens to police the park and to prevent local people from poaching the animals. To aid them in their game-keeping the Wardens had ten horses, two packs of dogs, and fifty-two spaniels.

It had been King John who, also in 1207, had transformed a tiny, obscure fishing hamlet of just a few families, then named 'Leverpul', into the burgeoning town, port, and borough that became known as Liverpool (it did not become a city until 1880). This would go on to become one of the fastest growing towns in Europe, and the 'second city of the

King John presents Liverpool with his Letters Patent or 'Charter' as a town, port, and borough. (Discover Liverpool Library)

British Empire' after London. It also became a major centre for the use and exploitation of all kinds of animals. However, the entire areas on both sides of the River Mersey were originally the location of agricultural and fishing communities.

## The Fisherfolk of Merseyside

The consumption of fish was an important part of life from the time of the first settled human communities. Of course, there was absolutely no pollution of water, land, or air at that time. This meant that the sea, the wide waterways of the Dee and the Mersey, and many small rivers and streams that criss-crossed the land were all filled with an abundance of fish of all species.

There was also an extensive supply of shellfish, broadening considerably the range of food available to the people. In particular, fishermen took to the Dee and the sea from Hoylake on Wirral; cockle pickers worked the Wallasey shore, especially around New Brighton; and prawns and shrimps provided significant income for the people of Neston, Parkgate, and Heswall. All these people sold their produce all over Wirral.

Whilst there was plenty of fish, at first people had no idea about how to catch them and caught only eels. They did not yet understand different methods of fishing, nor of preparation, storage, and cooking fish. As man developed and learned these new skills, so their societies became more sophisticated and organised. Fishing communities first used only lines and hooks, but later rods. They also used spears to hunt fish in shallower waters or pools. However, this was not very efficient, and it was the Roman and later Viking invaders who brought the use of nets to Britain, and to what would become Merseyside.

Medieval river fishermen.
(Liverpool Athenaeum Library)

First, these were used to block off parts of streams and rivers to trap the fish. Then the casting of nets developed to scoop them in large numbers. First these were cast from the shoreline and, later, from aboard small vessels such as hollowed-out logs and, later, coracles. Very soon larger boats were built that became the more familiar fishing boats of medieval history and later. Taking boats out to sea, or on rivers, was a significant technological advancement as expertise developed in the use of nets, as was the making and repairing of the nets themselves.

In the later thirteenth century, as the town of Liverpool grew, so fishing became more of an industry. Fleets of fishing boats now plied the Mersey and Liverpool Bay, catching enough to supply not only the needs of its own people, but also those of towns and villages right across the north-west of England. Liverpool's fish markets began to thrive, and now fishermen and the town became wealthier. This was because they could charge virtually whatever they liked for their catches as demand was so high. As a by-product this funded the shipbuilding industry on both sides of the Mersey.

As well as harvesting shellfish or catching fish wild, by the Middle Ages the farming of fish had developed. This was first begun by communities of monks, especially the Benedictine and the Cistercian orders. They created fish farms (fisheries) at various locations around Merseyside, especially at Stanlawe (Stanlow) on Wirral, and at Garston, just to the south of Liverpool. These latter fisheries were particularly extensive and profitable, providing shrimps and flatfish, and later trout, for home consumption and for sale in the district and at the markets in Liverpool.

Monks from Garston also bred pigs on land at what is now Speke. The name of this community derives from the Anglo-Saxon word 'Spic', which means 'bacon'. The fish farms of Garston operated on the broad mudflats of that part of the river; the part of modern Garston that stretches from under the railway bridge to the coast. That is why people who live in that area (including myself and my family) are known as 'the mud people' or 'mud-men'.

Even as late as 1918 we see fishermen mending their nets in Liverpool's Albert Dock. (Discover Liverpool Library)

As Liverpool became a major port for international maritime trade, especially in the nineteenth century, the local fishing industry faded in importance. Even so, some fishing families and small companies continued operating out of the port until the 1920s and 1930s. Fishing boats continued to sail from Hoylake and West Kirby though, until after the Second World War, and from Parkgate and Neston until the shore there began to silt up and become unnavigable.

## Of Sperm, Bowhead, and *Moby Dick*

Liverpool in particular, as well as the rest of Merseyside, benefitted from the 'fruits of the sea' in many ways. This was not only from the very smallest of creatures, the shrimps and prawns, but also from the most impressive sea creatures of all, the great whales.

From around 1750 until the early decades of the nineteenth century, whaling was a vital part of the maritime economy of Liverpool. Hunting these mammoth creatures – for oil, meat, and for precious and rare ambergris – demanded courage, incredible strength, and stamina from whale hunters. Endurance was also vital, especially in the storm-tossed and icy waters of the seas around Greenland and Iceland, which was the main destination of Liverpool whalers.

Most of all though, endless patience was required. This was because weeks or sometimes months might pass before the waterspouts of their prey were sighted. Then, the lookout would give the cry that lifted the hearts of the profit-hungry and risk-driven seafarers: 'There she blows!'

Whaling ships generally travelled in small fleets with anything between forty and 140 crewmen on each vessel. When the hunt was called every ship in the fleet lowered longboats. The six to twelve men in each of these then rowed, at breakneck speed, after the schools of sea-giants. In the prow of each of these stood the most important and, after the captain, the highest-paid members of the crew, the harpooners. It was their responsibility to hurl the heavy, long, barbed spear into the whale, with sufficient power to maim and then kill the creature.

Whilst the sperm whale was significantly hunted by international whaling fleets, ships from Liverpool principally targeted the *Balaena mysticetus,* better known as the bowhead whale. Also known as the Greenland whale, the common whale, and the Arctic whale, Liverpool whalers called it the 'right whale'. This was because, after the blue whale, which is the largest animal ever known to have existed, the right whale was the biggest in terms of weight.

It carried plenty of blubber up to 19 inches thick, and great sheets of baleen or 'whalebone' in its mouth. Also, the animal was rather slow, timid, and therefore easy to catch. This, and the fact that it stayed afloat after it had been killed, clearly made it the 'right' whale to hunt.

With a natural lifespan of around 200 years, the bowhead is named because of its massive bow-shaped head. It uses this to ram through sheets of ice up to 2 feet thick. They feed by swimming with their mouths gaping wide open to catch up to 2 tons of plankton daily; in fact, their mouths make up one-third of their body length. Eighteenth-century whalers declared that a bowhead's maw was big enough to take a ship's longboat, together with its crew and all their equipment.

The longboat approaches and the harpooner takes aim. (Discover Liverpool Library)

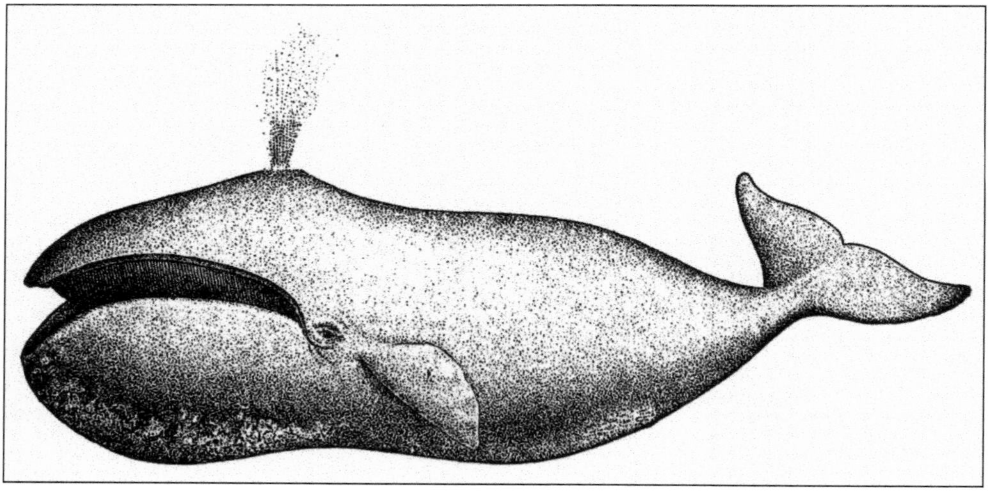

Bowhead or Right whale.

A whale of 60 feet in length could yield up to 30 tons of oil from blubber, which lit the lamps and lubricated the machinery of the Industrial Revolution (*c.* 1760–*c.* 1830). Whale meat was eaten, as was blubber, which was also used in the manufacture of varnish, explosives, paint, soap, leather goods, and even margarine up to the 1930s.

Another product of whaling was ambergris. This hard, waxy, inflammable substance is found in the digestive systems of some sperm whales and is a sort of combination of potential vomit and potential faeces! It stinks. So, it is surprising that it was an essential ingredient in the costliest perfumes and exotic aphrodisiacs. Liverpool whalers sometimes hunted these animals too, especially if there were no bowheads around.

The industry reached its peak by 1788, when twenty-one vessels were registered in Liverpool as whalers. In that year, this fleet sailed for the Arctic and returned with the oil and blubber from seventy-six whales. Even the hold of a single vessel filled with barrels of whale oil would make its crew, its captain, but mostly its owners extremely wealthy.

Though profits were great, so too were the risks. Frequently, whales escaped their hunters, or turned on them and destroyed their longboats and their men. Indeed, in 1789, four whaling ships from Liverpool were lost at sea with all hands. In one famous case in 1820, the New England whaler *Essex* was destroyed by a mammoth white whale that sought it out and seemed to deliberately attack it. Only a few of its crew survived. In 2016, the story was told in the film *Heart of the Sea.*

From an original population of around 50,000 the bowhead was mercilessly hunted almost to extinction over the course of some 250 years. Eventually there were none to be found in the Greenland Sea. By 1827, the last permanent whaler operating out of the Port of Liverpool appears to have been a ship named *Baffin.* This had also been the first whaling ship to be built in the port, in 1820.

Even so, Herman Melville (1819–91), the American author, visited Liverpool in 1839. He was so inspired by the wonders of the port and its place in whaling history that, in 1851, he went on to write his great novel about whaling, *Moby Dick.* He also used the disaster of the *Essex* to shape his plot.

American author of *Moby Dick,* Herman Melville. (Discover Liverpool Library)

In this great yarn Melville tells of the driving and relentless search of Captain Ahab, aboard the whaling ship *Pequod*, for the 'great white whale' after whom the book is named. This had chewed off the captain's leg on a previous whaling expedition. At the start of the fateful voyage the obsessive captain arouses and exhilarates his men on deck:

> 'Aye, my hearties ... it was Moby Dick that dismasted me; Moby Dick that brought me to this dead stump I stand on now.'
>
> 'Aye, aye! And I'll chase him round Good Hope, and round the Horn, and round the Norway Maelstrom, and round perdition's flames before I give him up.'
>
> 'And this is what ye have shipped for, men! To chase that white whale on both sides of land, and over all sides of earth, till he spouts black blood and rolls fin out!'

In his search for revenge Ahab leads himself, his ship, and his crew to destruction in the jaws of his monstrous marine nemesis. In fact, as Moby Dick finally drags Ahab to his death below the waves, the drowning seaman shouts out to the creature, '... to the last I grapple with thee; from hell's heart I stab at thee; for hate's sake I spit my last breath at thee'.

The author of *Moby Dick* had arrived in Liverpool, directly from New York, on his first ever sea voyage and at the age of only twenty. He was working as a cabin boy aboard the *St. Lawrence*, and he stayed in the port for a month before sailing out again on the same vessel.

What he saw and experienced in the town moved, inspired, and shocked him, because this 'crossroads of the world' was a melting pot of all nations and cultures, and a pool of great wealth and abject poverty.

The whaling industry in Liverpool was, for a time, a major contributor to the town's growth. The culture and community associated with the trade also added to the character and the mythology of the port. Nevertheless, by the middle of the nineteenth century no more whalers sailed from Liverpool in pursuit of great whales – white or otherwise.

## Hale Duck Decoy

As well as creatures of the sea, man has hunted the creatures of the air too – again, for food, clothing, and other purposes. One of the most popular of these species were ducks, and one of the methods of trapping them was quite ingenious and, in many ways, beautiful: the Duck Decoy. An excellent example of this can be found close to the township of Hale, just to the south of Liverpool, and it is one of the most important historical and archaeological sites in Britain.

Lowland coastal areas of England, such as those still around Hale, were not only suitable for pasture in medieval and later times, but the seasonal flooding that takes place in them created marshes and pools that still attract wildfowl to the area.

For centuries, these birds provided an additional source of food that was important to the local community, and such was the case at Hale. Throughout England during the sixteenth and seventeenth centuries, and possibly inspired by the Dutch, what is an ingenious method of trapping ducks for food and feathers began to become established. The Hale Duck Decoy is one of the finest surviving examples of such a system.

There were 215 Duck Decoys recorded in 1868, mostly on the east coast of England, but only forty-four of these were working at that time. Today, only five such decoys

The Hale Duck Decoy seen from the air. (Discover Liverpool Library)

survive – all in nature reserves. However, there were only ever three in the North West, of which Hale is the only survivor.

Built in either 1613 or 1631 (records are unclear), it stands in the centre of what is known as 'Decoy Marsh' adjacent to Halegate Farm. The Hale Duck Decoy is a specially constructed, irregular, pentagonal pond. This is surrounded by a high, broad, wooded copse and a moat that is 16 feet wide. This is crossed by a swing bridge.

The decoy was designed to resemble other, natural coverts that were dotted around the surrounding landscape. These attracted hundreds of waterfowl that visited Hale Marshes annually to nest and breed – as they still do. The ducks were attracted to the decoy because it was secluded and sheltered, and they found the artificially created environment ideal for nesting, believing it to be no different from other nesting sites.

The layout of the Duck Decoy is particularly ingenious because it is made up of five channels that radiate out from the central pond, and which are brick-lined. These are called 'pipes' and are caged over with hoops that are spaced out and covered with netting. From the air the decoy looks like a large hexagonal star with five curved arms.

The mouth of the pipe faces the pond and is a semicircle of about 10 to 15 feet in circumference. This is so large that it remains unnoticeable from the duck's point of view. This means that they swim from the pond into the channels, unaware that they are entering the fat end of a watery wedge. Each pipe is 150 feet long and bends out of sight into the woodland, so that the birds do not realise that these lead nowhere, except into suddenly narrowing points with trap-nets at the end. These are hidden in the bushes and trees on the bank.

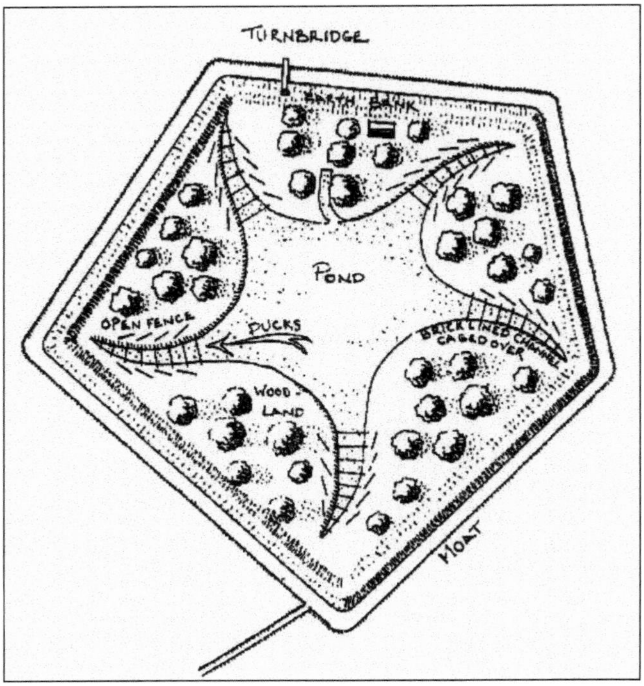


*Left*: This plan shows the design of the artificial duck pond.

*Below*: The mouth of the 'pipe' opens directly onto the central pond. (Discover Liverpool Library)

Between each pipe are small areas of additional woodland and, when the decoy was working, the channels were fenced on both sides, in a zigzag pattern, by separate slatted screens or closely woven osier fences, each 11 feet high.

These had small holes cut in them, at intervals, so that a duck hunter could stand concealed behind them, at the broad end of the trap, and upwind from the nesting birds.

Ducks always fly into the wind when taking off, so having five pipes positioned around the pond gave flexibility to the hunter to set his trap, always against the wind. The birds unwittingly swam into the mouths of the pipes, as the hunter watched and waited behind the wooden boards with his special breed of dog.

These dynamic little canines were trained to run between the zigzag boards, to draw ducks deeper into the trap, and the birds were usually further encouraged to continue down the pipe by the hunter's assistants beating on the fences. The ducks then flew deep into the pipe until they reached the hunter's nets at the end, where they were easily bagged.

Interestingly, it seems that far from flying away from the dogs the ducks flew or swam towards them. This was because they regarded the barking creatures as small predators, so they wanted to drive them away from their nests in the pond. This meant that the dogs acted as lures as opposed to terriers.

The dogs used by the hunters were a specific breed known as 'Duck Toller', and these were chosen particularly for their colour, which resembled that of a fox, and so this would appropriately panic the ducks. Between 750 and 1,500 ducks could be caught each season, making the Hale Duck Decoy a highly effective and sophisticated hunting system.

Although disused and derelict for many years, today the decoy is still a haven for ducks. This follows a major restoration and reclamation of the pond and its surrounding woodlands. Also, one or two of the pipes, channels, and nets have also been fully repaired and rebuilt. The surrounding moat has also been cleaned up and de-silted, and its banks renewed and strengthened.

In the autumn, the decoy can attract an average of 800 teal and 400 mallard. In the spring, around 100 sheldrake can be found at any given time nesting on the pond. However, the birds are perfectly safe as the decoy will never again be used for its original purpose, as it is now a scheduled ancient monument.

Duck hunter hiding behind screens with his Duck Toller Retriever. (Liverpool Athenaeum Library)

# 2. A Sporting Life and Death

Back in the days of developing tribes and communities of hunter-gatherers, animals were hunted and killed as a matter of necessity. From the animals' point of view however, humans seemed to enjoy this too much. So much indeed, that they began hunting and killing for entertainment or for sport, and to satisfy almost atavistic urges to dominate and destroy.

As tribes settled, and as villages and then towns developed, agriculture became organised and the need for food and fur became an established and systemised process; farming and animal husbandry became the norm. The animals we 'needed' were now largely domesticated; however, this did not satiate humanity's primitive desire for hunting and killing.

However, to demonstrate that we had risen above our primitive, wanton heritage, we now legitimised this in a more 'modern' and 'civilised' context. We did so by organising our hunting into often ritualised forms of 'sporting activity'. Nevertheless, and despite often legitimate justifications such as 'disease and population control', these human versus animal activities were, and in most cases remain, killing for killing's sake. Often, and even if the animals do not die, these activities are also torturing for torturing's sake.

From the Middle Ages people needed no justification for taking pleasure in depriving an animal of its life in the most violent and painful ways. Such organised activities included cockfighting, ratting, dog fighting, game hunting and shooting, deer stalking, fox hunting, and hare coursing. Then there was baiting.

## Bears, Bulls, and Baiting

A popular pastime in and around Liverpool in the seventeenth and eighteenth centuries was the baiting of tethered animals – specifically bears and bulls. Using a 15-foot-long rope or chain, a single animal was fastened by the neck or leg, or by the horns, to a stake that had been secured into the ground.

The larger and fiercer the animal the better, as far as the audience were concerned, because this made for a more entertaining show. The big animal was first harassed and tormented, and then attacked by barking, snarling dogs, either singly or in a pack. This took place in front of the cheering and baying crowds of people, most of whom had bet money on the outcome. Baiting took place either in specially built arenas or in pits, compounds, or other suitable places that allowed for large crowds of spectators.

Often, a baiting was stopped before serious or permanent injury was done to either bear, bull, or dogs, so that all animals could be made to fight again later. In this way even more money could be bet, won, or lost on the outcome. Generally, though, the vicious and very bloody battles only ended when the bear overcame the dogs using its claws and muzzle, or the bull did so with its horns and hooves, or when the snarling dogs had savaged and overpowered the larger animal.

Baiting a chained bear with ravenous dogs. (Discover Liverpool Library)

This was frequently the case because there were generally six to eight dogs in an attack pack that could move about freely, whilst their single victim remained tethered and with extremely restricted movement. Dogs were specially bred for this purpose, hence 'bulldog' and 'bull terrier'.

From the seventeenth century, bear baiting was held near the ruins of ancient Liverpool Castle at what is now Derby Square. From the mid-eighteenth century, to celebrate the annual election of a new mayor for the town, every October at the top of Chapel Street a chained bear was baited with large mastiffs. The bear was attacked separately one dog after another, and the most 'courageous' dog was rewarded with a special brass collar.

To really entertain the local populace, a previously blinded bear was placed in a circle of five or six men, who then proceeded to mercilessly whip the creature, often to death. In the late eighteenth century there was also a bull-baiting arena at the top of Lord Street.

## Cocks and Dogs

For centuries, setting specially trained fighting or 'game' cocks against each other in vicious battles, generally in pairs, was one of the most popular sports in England. This was especially true from the mid-sixteenth century through to the late-nineteenth century, and it appealed to people of all classes of society. The 'sport' was particularly popular on Wirral, in North Cheshire, and in south Lancashire (including Liverpool). Indeed, Lancashire cocks were internationally famous for their strength and tenacity.

Male cocks with an instinctive aggression towards each other were trained to fight by highly-skilled and often well-paid breeders. As well as using their claws and beaks as weapons, they were also equipped with long, thin, curved spurs, attached to their legs. The birds used these to slash at their opponents until one was victorious.

Squawking, feathers, and blood filled the air and excited the spectators to heights of frenzy that matched those of the birds. Various amounts of money were gambled on the outcome, and fortunes could be won or lost in a matter of minutes – cockfights were fast and furious affairs.

These battles took place outdoors and inside too, but generally involved a circular arena with a sand or beaten earth floor, roughly 20 feet in diameter. This was enclosed by a barrier on which the first of many rows of spectators usually leaned. Contests were known as either 'Cocking-Mains', involving fights between an agreed number of pairs of birds, or as 'Battles Royal', in which any number of birds were placed in the pit at the same time until all but one, the 'victor', were killed or disabled.

In Liverpool there were many cockpits throughout the town and its surrounding communities, including in the districts of Wavertree, Aintree, Knowsley, Old Swan, and in the nearby market town of Prescot. In fact, regular contests were fought here between cocks from Knowsley and Liverpool, which brought crowds of spectators and 'sportsmen' from miles around.

In the centre of Liverpool there were several cockpits: on the north shore, near what is now Waterloo Dock; on the present site of Lime Street Station; where the Picton Library now stands, on William Brown Street; where St George's Hall now stands; and in what is now Cockspur Street (hence the name) off Pall Mall.

Fighting cocks in full force.

Cockfighting was accessible to all, regardless of social class or personal income, but it was particularly enjoyed by the aristocracy and landed gentry. In the region at that time there were two genuinely great aristocratic families who each owned vast estates. The first of these was the Molyneux family, the Earls of Sefton, whose family seat was at Croxteth Hall and Park, near West Derby. Their line died out with the 7th Earl in 1972. The second great family were (and remain) the Stanleys, the Earls of Derby. The 19th and current Earl resides and thrives at Knowsley Hall and Park, to the east of Liverpool.

Both families enjoyed many sports that involve animals (as shall be seen), including cockfighting. Indeed, whilst on his deathbed in 1736, the 10th Earl of Derby watched a cockfight on the floor of his bedroom. On his orders and in defiance of Lady Derby, a footman had hauled a pair of fighting cocks in wicker baskets up through the Earl's bedroom window, on the end of a rope!

Edward Smith-Stanley (1752–1834), 12th Earl of Derby, was an exceptionally wealthy individual who enjoyed gambling, especially at cards and at the cockpits. He bred his own fighting cocks, known famously as 'The Knowsley Breed', and a famous fighting cock, *The Derby Red*, was named after him. The Earl also owned several cockpits himself, at Knowsley and Prescot, and in Liverpool and Preston. At his house at Newmarket, near Cambridge in Suffolk, known as Stanley House, the Earl even had a cockpit installed under his dining table. This was for the entertainment of his guests but also so that, whilst all were eating, he would still have the opportunity to win money from them, although Lord Derby frequently lost too!

Baiting a bull with dogs, cheered on by a frenzied crowd. (Discover Liverpool Library)

Prize money at cockfights could be considerable, and competition between owners and breeders was intense. This was as true for the lowliest workman or farmer with only one or two birds as it was for the very wealthiest owners who had dozens of birds in their 'stables'. Indeed, in 1789, advertisements in local newspapers announced:

> 'A main of cocks to be fought in the North Shore Cockpit on 12th May 1789, for 20 guineas a battle [almost £4,000 today] and £200 [£30,000 today] the main or odd battle. To show fifty cocks each.'
>
> 'A main of cocks to be fought at the new cockpit in Cockspur Street on 23rd June 1789, for Thirty Pounds [almost £5,000 today] a battle and £300 [£46,000 today] the main or odd battle. To show 41 cocks.'

Also, over four days in 1790, two Lancashire families fought Mains involving forty-one individual cockfights. The winner of each match received ten guineas (£2,000), with 200 guineas going to the overall winner.

In 1830, cocks owned by Lord Derby took on birds owned by a breeder named John Gilliver for an incredible stake of £5,000 (£760,000 today!).

Cockfighting was banned in 1849 but continued as an underground sport. In fact, according to a report by the RSPCA, published in 2007, cockfighting in England and Wales was still taking place.

Cockpits were also used for dog fighting, which grew considerably in popularity throughout the early to mid-nineteenth century. This also involved the use of specially trained and bred animals, and pairs of these instinctively aggressive dogs were pitted (hence the word) against each other. Whilst death was less the outcome in these battles, severe maiming and injury were the invariable outcome for both animals.

Breeds of fighting dogs included, perhaps obviously, the pit bull, American bulldog, Doberman, and German shepherd. As well as Rottweiler and Akita. Dog fighting, bear baiting, and bull baiting were officially outlawed in England by the Humane Act of 1835. However, this was regularly flouted, and, in fact, dog fighting continues underground in Britain today.

Whilst all the 'sports' involving animals that I have just described have now (largely) passed into history in this country, this is not the case for other organised assaults on various species of animals. A number of these remain popular and active across the region, especially amongst the more 'monied' classes of our society. These hunting parties have become traditional over time and are named 'field sports'. They took (and in some cases still take) several forms, and all have their part to play in the history of man and animal on Merseyside.

## Huntin' an' Shootin'

Perhaps the most traditionally British field sport is fox hunting, which had reached its modern, recognisable form by the late eighteenth century. This was popular on Wirral and in and around Liverpool. In fact, the Liverpool Hunt used to assemble outside the Coffee House pub that still stands at the heart of Wavertree Village. It was here that the pre-hunt drink of a glass of sherry or port was passed to the huntsmen once they had mounted their steeds.

This 'stirrup cup' was taken before the hunt set off across the once rural Childwall Heath and the surrounding countryside. In the words of playwright Oscar Wilde (1854–1900), 'The unspeakable in pursuit of the uneatable'!

Hunting foxes is a sport that involves the tracking, chasing and, if caught, the killing of a fox, traditionally by a pack of around sixty trained foxhounds or other scent hounds. The animal hunted in such a way is the red fox (*Vulpes vulpes*), and the dog pack leads a traditionally dressed number of huntsmen and women on horseback. There are often also many 'followers' on foot. The hunt is led by a 'Master of Foxhounds'.

Traditional fox hunting with hounds, as a formalised sport, continued until February 2005, when the Hunting Act 2004 came into force. This made the traditional style of 'hunting wild mammals with a pack of dogs (three or more)' unlawful in England and Wales. A ban on hunting in Scotland had been passed in 2002, but at the time of writing it continues to be within the law in Northern Ireland, as well as in several other countries around the world.

The ban was highly contentious, with supporters of hunting saying that it was an important part of rural culture, and useful for reasons of conservation, pest control, and employment. Indeed, in the lead-up to the Parliamentary debates on the subject a number of hunt-supporter marches took place. One of these involved nearly half a million people.

However, opponents of fox hunting and other 'blood sports' were just as vocal and active, stating that this was cruel and unnecessary, and totally out of place in a modern society and culture. One supposes that it would be perhaps easier to accept hunting supporters' arguments if they did not seem to derive such pleasure and a sense of accomplishment from the act of killing itself. They take such pride in depriving a creature of life in the name of 'sport'.

Modern huntsmen and huntswomen in traditional garb.

Despite the new legislation, hunts continued to take place in Britain following artificially laid trails or using exemptions laid out in the Act. Even so, the League Against Cruel Sports, founded in 1924, has alleged that breaches of the law are taking place by some hunts. Supporters of fox hunting agree that the number of foxes killed since 2005 has increased, but only by the hunts using lawful methods and by landowners and farmers killing foxes as vermin – although, foxes have never legally been classed as such.

Currently, and despite the ban, hunts have seen an increase in membership, and the Masters of Foxhounds Association (MFHA) currently represents 176 active foxhound packs in England and Wales and ten in Scotland.

As well as fox hunting, for centuries certain gentry had organised groups of their family members, friends, and other guests to go shooting animals on their land. Their targets included partridge and grouse, rabbits, and deer. These 'shooting parties' were held on most of the large, privately owned estates across Merseyside, especially during the seventeenth, eighteenth, and nineteenth centuries.

Such lands included the Old Hutte Estate at Halewood and on Hale Marshes, both the property of the Ireland and Blackburne families. Shoots were also held on land in Liverpool owned by wealthy politician Bamber Gascoyne Esq. (1758–1824), and later the Marquesses of Salisbury, at Woolton, Gateacre, Childwall, and Wavertree.

Hunting of all kinds also took place on the great parkland owned by the Molyneux and the Stanley families. Both ancient dynasties were great sportsmen and, as we shall see, the Earls of Derby founded the Oaks and the Derby horse races, and the Earls of Sefton helped to establish the Waterloo Cup for Hare Coursing and the Grand National Steeplechase.

'Lord Dashalong', 2nd Earl of Sefton. (Liverpool Athenaeum Library)

Sir William Philip Molyneux (1771–1838), the 2nd Earl of Sefton, was known as 'Lord Dashalong' because of his fondness for recklessly driving a carriage and four about the streets of Liverpool. He extended his Croxteth Hall mansion and developed and managed his Croxteth parkland estate principally for field sports. This now became a famous shooting estate, where over 1,000 pheasants could be shot in one day.

During the Victorian and Edwardian eras, the Croxteth Hunting weekends became increasingly popular and well attended by royalty, international aristocracy, and by celebrities of the day. They also became notorious for their excesses, self-indulgences, and for the flaunting of great wealth in an otherwise extremely poor and deprived part of Britain.

After the death of the 7th and last Earl of Sefton, in 1972, the estate passed to Liverpool City Council and obviously all field sports then ceased completely. The hall and the estate are now open to the public. Knowsley Hall, though, remains in the ownership of the Stanleys, and game bird shoots are still provided for Lord Derby's family and friends. These are also offered to paying guests and for corporate events to generate income for the estate. Shoots take place in October, November, December, and January, and often bag from 200 to 300 birds a day.

The present Lord Derby's website explains that 'the parkland offers a range of drives ... providing the guns with a varied and satisfying days sport. We can offer a day shoot, with the guns arriving in the morning, or alternatively guests can opt for a residential shoot, where the guns arrive the evening prior to the days shooting.'

Edwardian gamekeepers on Lord Sefton's estate at Croxteth Hall. (Discover Liverpool Library)

In Britain what officially constitutes 'game' is defined by the Game Act 1831. Other (non-game) birds that are hunted for food across the country are specified under the Wildlife and Countryside Act 1981. The law in England, Scotland, and Wales specifically defines game and their respective hunting seasons as:

| | |
|---|---|
| Pheasant | 1 October–1 February |
| Partridge, grey and red-legged | 1 September–1 February |
| Black Grouse | 20 August–10 December |
| Red Grouse | 12 August–10 December |
| Ptarmigan | 12 August–10 December |
| Brown hare (Lepus europaeus) | No closed season (may be killed at any time) |

Similar controls provided to those under the Game Act also apply to deer in the Deer Act 1991. Deer hunted in Britain are: red deer, roe deer, fallow deer, sika deer, muntjac deer, Chinese water deer, and hybrids of these deer.

Ducks and geese shot as game in the UK include: mallard, wigeon, teal, shoveler, pintail, common pochard, common goldeneye, gadwall, and tufted duck, greylag goose, Canada goose, pink-footed goose, and (in England only) white-fronted goose.

Also shot as game are wood pigeon, woodcock, snipe, golden plover, and rabbit. Black grouse and capercaillie are no longer shot because of their declining numbers. Animals that can be shot as vermin are feral pigeon, jay, magpie, carrion crow, jackdaw, rook, and collared dove.

## Run Rabbit Run!

Another extremely popular hunting sport on Merseyside was hare coursing. This involved two or three greyhounds trying to catch hares that were released from traps into a large open field, generally enclosed by hedges. The hare was given a short head start, then the dogs were released to pursue them at great speed. If the hare made it to and through the hedge at the far end of the field then it escaped, because the dogs could not follow it. If, however, the dogs caught it, they then tore the hare to pieces, with their tragic victims often taking several minutes to die.

The first modern hare coursing club in England had been founded in 1776, but what became an annual three-day Merseyside event was the idea of a Liverpool innkeeper and entrepreneur named William Lynn (1794–1872). In 1836, he sponsored the first hare coursing event at Altcar, not far from Ormskirk in Lancashire, on land owned by the 2nd Earl of Sefton. Lynn named his event 'The Waterloo Cup' after his popular and luxurious Waterloo Hotel, then standing on Ranelagh Street in Liverpool. Lynn saw this event as a way to increase revenue for this and for his other enterprises, and in this he was remarkably successful.

Lynn's first Altcar meeting attracted huge crowds. It was won by a greyhound bitch named Melanie, which was owned by Lord Molyneux, the eldest son of the Earl of Sefton. As well as winning prize money of £16 (£1,840), the aristocrat was awarded a silver snuffbox as a trophy.

The event soon became so popular that it was attracting crowds of up to 75,000 people from across Britain. It was the biggest annual hare coursing event in the United Kingdom, and was often referred to by its supporters as the 'Blue Riband' event of the coursing year.

William Lynn's Waterloo Hotel in Liverpool. (Liverpool Athenaeum Library)

The first supreme champion greyhound in hare coursing was named Master McGrath and was owned by Lord Lurgan. The dog won the Waterloo Cup in 1868, 1869, and 1871, and he became famous around Britain. So much so that the greyhound was commanded to make an appearance before Queen Victoria at Windsor Castle.

Nevertheless, by the mid-1960s, the calls were getting louder for hare coursing, fox hunting, and other blood sports to be declared illegal. The League Against Cruel Sports mounted effective campaigns to draw public attention to the horrors of hunting and coursing. They were joined by the RSPCA, who condemned the Waterloo Cup meeting as barbaric, and they gained support, not just from the public, but from significant celebrities, including Sir Paul McCartney (b. 1942).

Eventually, hare coursing was finally banned in Britain by the Hunting Act 2004. However, at the time of writing, it continues illegally in counties with large areas of flat farmland, including Lincolnshire, Cambridgeshire, and Norfolk.

Hare coursing at Altcar before the sport was banned.

# 3. The Sport of Kings

Two of humanity's less controversial animal-centred sports are racing with greyhounds and whippets, and horse racing. Modern greyhound racing, which became established in the early decades of the twentieth century, was an evolution of hare coursing that used a mechanical lure.

At these events dogs race around an enclosed oval track, chasing what was originally a dummy hare but that was later replaced by a windsock. This runs along a metal track on the inside perimeter of the course and it has a few seconds start on the dogs, which are released from traps. The first such race in Britain was held, in 1926, at Belle Vue Stadium in Manchester.

Greyhound racing was extremely popular on Merseyside, especially in Liverpool, and there were four dog tracks in the city. These were Breck Park (founded in 1927, closed by 1950), White City Greyhound Stadium (founded 1927, closed in 1973), Stanley Greyhound Stadium (opened 1927, closed in 1961), and Seaforth Greyhound Stadium (opened in 1933, closed 1965). There was also a track at Ellesmere Port that opened in the late 1960s and closed in 2014.

However, it is horses that take part in what are the longest-established, officially organised animal races in Britain. Enjoyed by the public and the working man, the sport became, in many respects, a great equaliser, although horse racing was, and remains, a favourite activity of royalty and the aristocracy – hence it also being known as 'the Sport of Kings'.

## Merseyside's Horse Racing Pioneers

We met the ancient and powerful Stanley family earlier, and they had been enobled as the Earls of Derby, in 1485, by King Henry VII (1457–1509). As a result, they became immensely wealthy, and went on to own lands and property around Britain. They also held great houses and lodges in London; in Surrey; in Scotland; at Lathom, near Ormskirk; Bidston, on the Wirral; and at Knowsley, to the east of Liverpool, which remains their family seat. They also owned the great, fortified Tower of Liverpool, which once stood in the town itself.

Over the centuries, the Stanley family played an important role in the life and politics of Britain, but they will forever be associated with the sport of horse racing, particularly 'The Oaks' and the 'Epsom Derby' races. Their connection with the 'Sport of Kings' and with the breeding of racehorses can be traced back to the time of Ferdinando Stanley (1559–94), the 5th Earl of Derby.

It was he who, in 1593, built a large, octagonal tower on the shore near Wallasey, which was then a small village on the north-east coast of the Wirral Peninsula; four storeys tall this later became known as Leasowe Castle. It was from the roof and upper floors of this tower that Earl Ferdinando and his friends organised and watched the regular, and increasingly popular, Wallasey races. These were run along the sands and heathlands of the shore.

Ferdinando Stanley, 5th Earl of Derby. (Discover Liverpool Library)

Although the sea has now encroached much further inland, these 'leasowes' or meadows along the shoreline of what were then the tiny communities of Wallasey, Leasowe, Moreton, and Meols Sands may well have been one of the oldest formal racecourses in England. A description of the Wallasey beaches from that time says, 'Those flat sands or plains upon the shore of the seas, which for the fitness of such a purpose, allure gentlemen and others to try the swiftness of their horses.'

The shore at Leasowe today, along which the first local horse races were run in the sixteenth century. (Discover Liverpool Library)

Naturally, the racetrack at Wallasey was nothing like we understand modern racecourses to be. It was simply a long stretch of open land with no fences or barriers on either side, and with only some tall, wooden posts set out at long intervals to guide the jockeys along the route, which ran for over 5 miles.

This was extremely taxing for both the animals and the jockeys. Especially so, because, if the first horse past the winning post (or 'distance chair' as it was also known) was not at least 240 yards ahead of the second horse, then the whole race had to be run again – or even for a third time.

William Stanley (*c.* 1561–1642) became the 6th Earl of Derby on the premature death of his brother. He was also a very keen supporter of the races at Wallasey and was an acknowledged expert on the sport. At this time horse races were being organised in other places across south Lancashire and North Cheshire too. In 1577, and as the sport became more popular, a race of approximately 4½ miles distance was held from Crosby to Bankhall, just to the north of Liverpool.

On 28 July 1627, James Stanley (1607–51), the 7th Earl of Derby, inaugurated a horse race on the Isle of Man, and which he named after himself – 'The Derby'. This first race was run on the Langness Peninsula on the Manx island, in an area that is still known as 'The Racecourse'. Official Manx records of the time note that the Earl awarded a cup as a trophy at these races.

Racing continued at Wallasey and, at a meeting there in the autumn of 1682, the Duke of Monmouth (1649–85) rode his own horse to victory along the shore, winning a first prize valued at £60 (£13,000) – it was suggested that the other jockeys reigned back their horses to allow the Duke to win.

By the early nineteenth century, the locations of regularly held races had spread. In the diary of Nicholas Blundell (1669–1737), the Lord of the Manor of Little Crosby, we read of him attending races in Great Crosby, Crosby Marsh, Ormskirk, Aughton Moss, Childwall, Knowsley Park, and on Liverpool Sands. Most frequently he attended the races run in Crosby and, from as early as November 1702, he writes of a 'Stand' for spectators there, built by Lord Molyneux.

It was at the Leasowe racecourse in 1723, and now under the supervision of James Stanley (1664–1736), the 10th Earl of Derby, that the first 'sweepstakes' were run, and the Leasowe races became known as 'The Wallasey Stakes'.

A sweepstake was a race in which the owner of each entered horse had to pay an equal amount of money, or 'stake', into the race fund. This was then awarded to the owner of the winning animal. The term comes from the winner who 'sweeps' or takes all the stakes in a race. When any group, or 'syndicate', of people – racehorse owners or otherwise – stake money on a race they become 'stakeholders'.

This principal still forms the core of modern race betting and, if an owner's horse runs but falls, his stake money is forfeit. However, if the horse is withdrawn before the start of the race, then a forfeit only is payable.

The 10th Earl took as keen an interest in horses and horse racing as his forefathers had. However, it was Edward Smith-Stanley III (1752–1834), the 12th Earl, who was to become the member of the Stanley family most closely associated with the

Leasowe Castle in the nineteenth century, showing Lord Derby's original octagonal tower. (Discover Liverpool Library)

'Sport of Kings'. By the early eighteenth century a racing ground had been established within Knowsley Park at which regular meetings were held. The Earl's impact on the sport, and his legacy, still shape horse racing and the breeding of racehorses today.

## Great Championships and Champions

Between the mid-1600s and the mid-1700s, the sport of horse racing had become more organised. Aristocrats and the wealthier classes had both the time and the resources to invest in a pastime that provided them with excitement and entertainment, recognition and honour, enhanced social status and influence, and a new source of income.

Wealthy patrons, including the Earls of Derby, were not only entering horses into other people's races, but were now organising their own. They were doing so either, like Lord Derby, on racecourses laid out on their own estates, or by making land available for race meetings, and by providing financial sponsorship or prize money.

Those sportsmen, like the Stanleys, who were now also breeding their own horses, were not only investing in their own stake in the sport but were actively increasing the quality of the bloodstock. By doing so, they were adding quality, value, and sustainability to a spectator sport that was soon to develop, almost, into an industry.

In 1750, the 'Jockey Club' was founded by racing enthusiasts who were determined to bring high standards and organisation to the sport. Specifically established to ensure that races on Newmarket Heath, in Suffolk, were run fairly, the club proved to be effective and popular amongst owners and breeders, and was appreciated by an increasingly discerning public.

This meant that their rules were gradually adopted at racecourses right across Britain. Eventually, the Jockey Club became what it remains, the official governing body of the sport. Then, one of the great developments in horse racing was about to take place, again, thanks to the 12th Earl of Derby.

Lord Derby had a country house just outside Epsom, in Surrey, named 'The Oaks'. It was here that he had the idea of creating a new horse race. This would be run over an exact, 1-mile-long, flat, straight, obstacle-free course across the Epsom Downs. To guarantee the fitness of the animals and so increase the excitement of the race, The Oaks was restricted to three-year-old fillies (young female horses) all carrying the same weight.

Named after his house, the Earl inaugurated 'The Oaks Stakes', which was first run on 14 May 1779. This was won by Lord Derby's own horse, Bridget, and the race proved to be instantly popular, becoming the annual 'Classic' racing event still being run today.

Following the success of The Oaks, the 12th Earl, at dinner with his friend Sir Charles Bunbury (1749–1821), was discussing the need for another new race. This would be run over the same course as The Oaks but would be open to three-year-old colts (young male horses) as well as to three-year-old fillies. Once they had agreed the criteria for the race,

Edward Smith Stanley (1752–1834), 12th Earl of Derby. (Discover Liverpool Library)

they had to decide on a name for it. Both gentlemen wanted to name it after themselves so, to settle the matter in true sporting tradition, they decided to toss a coin. Lord Derby won the toss, which is probably just as well, or what we now know as 'The Derby' might well have been called 'The Bunbury'!

The official name for this race became 'The Epsom Derby Stakes', and it was first run on 4 May 1780. Fortunately for Sir Charles, even though he had lost the coin toss, his horse, Diomed, resoundingly beat the rest of the field. The prize money was £1,065 and 15 shillings (£192,600), which was a considerable purse, and so, Sir Charles had another reason for celebration!

The Derby soon became the most popular horse race in the annual flat-racing season, which runs from the end of March until November. Winning this race is regarded, by owners and jockeys alike, as being a peak in a breeder's and a rider's career. As with other sporting fixtures, the name 'Derby' is now applied to several horse races on the flat around the world; but there is still only one, official, original 'Derby' horse race.

The 13th Earl of Derby (1775–1851), also named Edward Smith-Stanley, was another enthusiastic participant in field sports, especially those on horseback, such as stag hunting. In fact, some of the deer he bred at Knowsley were sent to The Oaks to be hunted across the Epsom Downs by the energetic guests at his house parties. Indeed, Earl Edward was just as keen on field sports as any of his ancestors had been, and he was often seen walking around his estate with his shotgun under his arm.

He was also a dedicated sportsman, a remarkable politician and statesman, and an outstanding collector and lover of live animals. We shall hear more about him and his amazing private zoo later, but he and his descendants continued the Stanley family commitment to horse racing and breeding. This includes the current and 19th Earl of Derby.

By the opening decades of the nineteenth century, horse racing had been established at Melling, just to the north of Liverpool. By 1829, this had transferred to nearby Aintree.

The Derby would become one of the leading 'Classic' horse races. (Discover Liverpool Library)

Because of this, the racecourse at Leasowe fell into disuse and neglect, as did Leasowe Tower, which then became known for a time as 'Mockbeggar Hall'.

However, a much-enlarged Leasowe Castle survives with the original octagonal tower still at its core, which is now a listed building. This has now been an attractive hotel for a few decades, today separated from the sea by a strong sea wall. Nevertheless, even in its current setting, and with the Irish Sea still providing a dramatic backdrop, it is easy to imagine those long-ago races along the beach.

Though the Wallasey races have long since disappeared, when one stands on the shore at Leasowe one can almost see again those majestic horses galloping along the sands and marram grassland whilst seagulls wheeled overhead. One can imagine their jockeys spurred on by the enthusiastic shouts from the owners and the ecstatic cheering of the spectators, with everyone totally absorbed in the thrill and passion of the chase.

It was at this time that Lord Derby and Lord Sefton, together with other horse breeders, owners, enthusiasts, and sporting speculators, established that other great annual event in the horse racing calendar, the 'Grand National Steeplechase'.

## 'Over the Sticks' – The Grand National

Towards the end of 1828, and almost a decade before he established the Waterloo Cup hare coursing event at Altcar, the enterprising Liverpool hotelier William Lynn had already had an inspirational idea to expand his business interests. Lynn knew that popular flat-races for horses had been running in the Melling and Maghull area of north Liverpool, near Altcar, from the previous year. However, he was convinced that he could organise these more effectively, and more profitably.

So, for financial backing, and as he would also do for his hare coursing events, he took his idea to the 2nd Earl of Sefton. Lord Sefton found Lynn's idea appealing and agreed to back him. The exceptionally wealthy aristocrat now made land available for a racecourse at nearby Aintree.

Lynn immediately enclosed a large area of this land and set out his new course. The foundation stone for the racetrack's first grandstand was laid by Lord Sefton, on 7 July 1829, and Lynn ran three flat-races that year alone. These annual race meetings became so successful that, by 1835, the Liverpudlian businessman had decided to make his Aintree races even more exciting by changing them into steeplechases. This form of horse race had already become increasingly popular because it was much more challenging and competitive than a race over flat ground.

The term 'steeplechase' comes from earlier times, before specialised racetracks were devised. This was when the horses raced across open country, over a fixed distance, literally from church steeple to church steeple. Such a race was also colloquially known as a race 'over the sticks' because the animals had to jump over whatever natural or man-made barriers they found in their way.

So, to replicate the hedges, brooks, and walls that horses encountered across open country, Lynn now built a series of fences and obstacles on his racecourse. His first Aintree steeplechase was held in 1836 and was an immediate triumph. The winner was Captain Martin Becher (1797–1864), riding The Duke, and very soon the race became known as 'The Grand Liverpool Steeplechase'.

By 1839, Lynn's annual Aintree steeplechase had now also become outstandingly popular and profitable. In that year, the race was formally renamed as 'The Liverpool and National Handicap Steeplechase' and, on 26 February, an estimated crowd of 50,000 spectators saw Lottery romp home as the undoubted winner. It was from then that the race became generally – but not officially – known as the 'Grand National'.

Lottery now entered into the record books as the first horse to win the famous Grand National Steeplechase. This animal was a great favourite with the crowd and seemed to enjoy all the attention; however, the horse absolutely hated his jockey, Jem Mason (1816–66). This meant that the rider had to creep up on the horse from behind, and quickly mount him before the animal realised who it was that was climbing onto his back!

Captain Becher was also riding in the 1839 race, on a horse named Conrad, but he fell into the 6-foot-wide brook at one of the fences. The Captain afterwards said that he 'Never knew water tasted so foul without whisky in it.' This jump has been known as 'Becher's Brook' ever since.

This obstacle is just one of the sixteen challenging fences faced by horses and jockeys alike as they make two circuits of the 2¼-mile-long course – although only thirty fences are ultimately jumped. Some of these are 'drop fences', where the landing side of the fence is lower than the take-off side. This means that the horses are unaware of the drop until they are in the air. However, the 'Chair Fence' has the opposite problem because the approach side is lower than the landing side! Also, the horses must negotiate some very tricky turns and then end the race with a 494-yard gallop to the winning post.

The race meeting continued to grow in popularity and financial success and, in 1847, it was renamed once again, now as the 'Grand National Handicap Steeplechase'. This is the name that it continues to hold officially today.

Up to 1949, the racecourse was owned by the Earls of Sefton, but in that year Lord Sefton sold it. Over subsequent decades, it passed through a variety of ownerships, with

The Grand National being run at Aintree in 1843.

the Grand National itself being sponsored by an equally varied range of companies. At the time of writing, the Grand National is now run by Jockey Club Racecourses, and the racecourse is owned by a charitable trust, of which the 19th Earl of Derby is a trustee.

Several exceptional horses have raced at Aintree, but perhaps the Grand National's most famous was Red Rum. He came second in the National in 1975 and 1976, and won it in 1973, 1974, and 1977. His grave, and a statue commemorating this extraordinary animal, are both sited at the racecourse.

However, whilst the Grand National is arguably the most famous horse race in the world, it is also the most controversial. In what has been described as 'the ultimate test of a horse's courage', as of 2022, and since its founding, there have been eighty-seven horse deaths over the 183-year period. The League Against Cruel Sports charity reports that since 2000, there have been fifteen deaths at the Grand National. Of forty horses that ran in the 2022 race only fifteen finished, and four animals died. (ITV News, 11 April 2022)

The campaigning animal rights organisation PETA UK says that the 'high risk factor is what makes The Grand National famous, but every year, horses lose their lives, sustaining horrific and often fatal injuries at notorious fences such as The Chair, Becher's Brook, and Canal Turn. Every time that horses are forced to jump these excessively high obstacles, it puts tremendous pressure on their slender front legs, leading to broken legs, necks, and backs.'

According to the Grand National's website though, 'Over the years Aintree race officials and the British Horse Racing Authority have introduced a number of safety-related changes to the Grand National to make the race safer.'

A modern steeplechase. (Hippodrome de Deauville – Clairefontaine)

# 4. Keeping Mankind Moving

As well as using animals for food, clothing, sport, etc., mankind domesticated and then bred entire species of animals for particular work and service. However, continuously over the millennia, it has been horses that have been utilised and exploited more than any other species, and in so many ways.

We have always used them for transportation, and have employed them in times of war, as we shall see later. Horses pulled our ploughs as we tilled the soil of our farms. In vast numbers they also provided motive power and traction for so many of our forms of wheeled transportation, together with donkeys, asses, and oxen. In particular, horses were used to power our machinery, until the invention of the steam engine.

It is undoubtedly true to say that without horses and their kind, humanity would not have the kind of civilisation or capacity for development that we have today – we owe it all to our exploitation of these strongest and most graceful of our domesticated animals, and to their 'horse power'.

In Britain, and excluding warfare, the use of horses began to increase exponentially by the end of the Middle Ages. There was a new surge in their use with the coming of the Agricultural Revolution (*c.* 1500 to 1850) and the Industrial Revolution (1760 to 1840).

Mankind depended on horses from the very earliest times.

## Of Pack, Cart, Stage, and Carriage

With the establishment of early villages, towns, and cities, ordinary people did not travel about the country very much at all. Generally, they were born, lived their entire lives, and died in the same places. Only the aristocracy and wealthier citizenry travelled about the country, and this was usually on horseback.

However, by the closing decades of the 1600s, increasing quantities of raw materials and manufactured goods were now being transported in and out of the town of Liverpool. This was first on habitually used packhorse trails or basic cart tracks.

Whilst transporting goods in this way was certainly less hazardous than doing so by sea around the coast, these inland routes were extremely poor and seldom maintained. They had been created over centuries of common use, and beaten flat by foot, hoof, and wheel. Most were rutted through overuse or overgrown because of irregular use. Many were also either full of potholes, completely flooded, or they washed away in bad weather.

Lone travellers or families who wished to travel out of Liverpool, with or without goods, faced these bad conditions. Robbers on these routes were a real threat, so there was 'greater security and strength in numbers'! Men travelled on horseback in small groups whenever possible, whilst women and children journeyed by cart or by hired carriage – that was if they had the money to pay for this service and for the men to escort and guard them en route.

By the beginning of the 1700s though, the most important road in and out of Liverpool was the packhorse route to the nearby market town of Prescot, just 8 miles to the east.

On the Liverpool to Prescot packhorse trail. (Discover Liverpool Library)

This trail was mainly travelled by long strings of burdened packhorses, carrying great sacks of coal. This had first been mined from shallow pits around the town, until demand saw the development of deep-mine coalfields around south Lancashire. There were often a dozen or more animals in a string, and around ten or twelve strings to a packhorse train.

Before long demand could not be met by packhorses, and now trains of horse-drawn coal carts had to replace them. This meant too that the roads had to be widened, improved, and maintained to support a developing economy. There was also a need for new routes to other places in the region and beyond.

To radically improve the quality of the coal route the government passed the Prescot Turnpike Act, 1726, and created the Liverpool to Prescot Turnpike Road. 'Turnpiked' meant that toll-booths, toll-gates, or toll-houses were placed at various points along a principal packhorse or coaching route, to raise income to pay for their regular maintenance.

A 'turnpike' itself was originally a gate-like frame, pivoting at one end on an upright post or 'pike'. This was used on roads to block the way until a toll was paid. Money raised was then spent on road maintenance and local constables to protect the routes.

The toll-keepers were called 'Pikemen', who wore a uniform. This consisted of a tall, black hat; black stockings and knee britches; and short aprons with deep pockets in which to hold the money. The pay to these men, and sometimes women, was poor, but at least they and their families could live, rent-free, in the purpose-built toll cottages.

By 1761, the new 'highway' was extended beyond Prescot to then connect with other major routes. This was now carrying the mail, goods, and news to and from Liverpool and Manchester, between the town and the Midlands, and then to London.

By 1785, and as mail services developed, soon people began to travel on the mail coaches. By the turn of the eighteenth and nineteenth centuries, coaches were now being built specifically for travellers and their luggage. Passengers began and ended their journeys at coaching inns and taverns in the main towns. Wealthy passengers were picked up at the gates of their mansions and houses, and the arrival of the coach was announced by the driver's 'post-horn'. Tolls were still being paid in addition to any fares people were paying to the carriers.

In the first decades of the nineteenth century travel became easier, safer, better organised, more available, and cheaper. Demand for more and better coaches increased, as it did for more new routes and roads. Increases in mail and passenger coaches meant many more journeys. This resulted in many more horses needing to be stabled, shod, fed, watered, and cared for.

Coaching inns were opening at an increasing number of coaching stops. These met the needs of passengers on long journeys, and alongside these appeared stables and blacksmiths workshops. These stops were near the toll gates and often only a mile or two apart, depending on how many hills the coaches and their horses had to cross. This is why the coaches were also known as 'stagecoaches', because the journey was completed in stages.

Coaches were dead weights being pulled by horses that were expected to maintain high speeds. As a result, a single coach, with often upwards of twenty people on board including the driver and his guard, often needed two animals to pull them or, more often, a team of four. Horses had to work particularly hard on the streets and roads of Liverpool. This was because the city is built on seven main hills and many smaller rises.

Liverpool mail and passenger stagecoach. (Discover Liverpool Library)

The profitability of a coaching route depended on the quality of healthy, strong animals that had to be frequently changed en route to keep them rested. This meant that they were worked extremely hard indeed, and often urged on with a whip, but the animals were generally well looked after – largely driven by profit rather for any genuine consideration for the well-being of the animals.

Nevertheless, by this time the age of horse-drawn carts and coaches travelling to other villages, towns, and cities was coming to an end. In early 1830, there were twenty-nine coaches regularly running between Liverpool and Manchester, but by 1831 there were four. By 1833, there were only two. This was because, in September 1830, the railways came to Britain and the world.

This radical technological development began in that year, with the inauguration of the Liverpool to Manchester steam railway. This was the world's first intercity passenger and goods railway, and it truly revolutionised transportation. Horses were required less and less, especially on long-distance routes, and society transformed fundamentally as a result. Even so, railways did not yet eliminate working horses entirely, as we shall see.

## Pulling Along the Cut

Before the coming of the railways, and even though the quality of roads had improved radically from the eighteenth century, the volume of goods that needed to be transported around Britain, as well as locally, meant that trains of packhorses or of horse carts were simply too inefficient. With the advent of the Industrial Revolution, what was then the greatest innovation in long-distance travel and bulk transportation of goods and commodities had arrived: Britain's magnificent canal system

The first canal, or 'cut' as these became colloquially known, in Britain was the Sankey Brook Navigation between St Helens and the Mersey which opened in 1757, although people believe that the Bridgewater Canal was the first true canal, which opened in

Canal horses had to be very strong to haul barges full of cargo.

1761, and this still runs between Manchester and Runcorn on the Mersey. The longest canal remains the Leeds and Liverpool Canal, which is 127 miles long. This opened in stages between 1774 and 1822, although an extension was added at the Liverpool end in 2009.

Incidentally, the first entirely man-made canal in the UK was the Newry Canal in Northern Ireland. This opened in 1741, and was built by Thomas Steers (*c.* 1672–1750), the great engineer who, in 1715, had built Liverpool's (and the world's) first enclosed commercial wet dock.

However, this was all before the development of steam-powered locomotion, so, once again, it was the horse that provided the motive power for canal barges, narrowboats, and flatboats. Canals were dug with a narrow pathway running along their edge. This was the 'towpath' from which the animals hauled the vessels. They did so by means of a long rope running between the horse's special collar and the prow of the barge. Each rope was often around 80 feet long but only lasted around six weeks because of the heavy wear and tear.

A well-fitted horse collar was especially important for a canal horse because they had to lean into it when starting from rest. This was because the hardest job for the horse was pulling away from a standing start but, once the boat was underway it often travelled some distance under its own momentum before another steady tow was needed. Having said this though, canal boats often carried loads of up to 30 tons at a time with only one horse towing it. This was around ten times the amount of cargo that was possible for a single horse pulling a cart on a road or track.

If the horse collar was old, worn, or incorrectly fitted then sore shoulders or skin abrasions could result for the animal. If the horse was injured, or simply overtired during a journey, caring boatmen could stable it at one of the many locks and warehouses alongside the canal, where the animal was treated and rested.

Generally though, horses were again well looked after. This made economic sense as they could cost anything up to £50 each to buy, which is the equivalent of around £10,000 today. Also, if the animal was ill then it could not pull your boat. Boatmen who treated their animals badly were rare, and were heavily fined if they were discovered.

At the end of the day, the horse would always be well fed, and generally on good-quality fodder containing clover, hay, straw, corn, beans, and peas. They were then often simply tied up alongside the canal overnight but were always settled immediately after tying up and before the boatmen had their own meal.

There was no specific breed of horse used on canals, and boatmen simply made use of whatever animal was available and seemed up to the job. Medium-sized horses were preferred as these had little difficulty negotiating low bridges over the canals or the narrow towpaths. Sometimes mules and donkeys were used instead.

If barges had to pass through a flight of locks on the route then canal and transportation companies often used larger breeds of horses, such as Clydesdales. This was because at each step the boats had to be started from a static position. The extra effort to repeatedly get them in motion again required a much stronger and more redoubtable animal.

Once the railways began to revolutionise goods and passenger transport throughout Britain (and ultimately the world), from 1830, the use of canal barges and their horses began to progressively diminish, especially at the turn of the nineteenth and twentieth centuries. Even so, horses were still regularly to be seen pulling canal boats as late as the 1950s, and the last working horse boat finished only in 1960. This was the *Parbold,* operated by H. & R. Ainscough Ltd of Burscough near Ormskirk.

## 'Move right down inside please!'

As the population of towns and cities grew, especially during the mid-to-late nineteenth century, internal public transportation systems were now needed. People no longer only required a service to occasionally carry them from one part of a conurbation to another; they now needed them to get to work every day, in the shops, offices, and factories that were fast becoming the norm in urban life. This required dependable and timetabled public transport services.

There were 'hansom cabs' (designed by Joseph Hansom) and 'hackney carriages' (hack – a horse for hire). These carried one, two, or three passengers side by side in relative comfort, and were drawn by a single horse. Also, there were 'short-stage' coaches carrying more people and drawn by two or four horses. However, these did not cover a wide range of routes and could be expensive, especially for ordinary, working people.

Liverpool's first horse-drawn 'omnibus' service was established on 12 May 1830. This ran regularly from the Town Hall, travelling through Edge Hill and across the Great Heath, and then via Old Swan, arriving at the Turk's Head Inn in Knotty Ash Village. The journey took 1½ hours, and the fares were 10d and 6d.

The 'bus' was pulled by three horses and carried twenty-two passengers inside the vehicle, so they were protected from the weather. Omnibuses now ran to a strict timetable regardless of how many passengers they were carrying. They also picked up and set down passengers on request, anywhere along the clearly defined route. Also, fares were collected on board rather than being booked and paid for in advance, as on board short-stage coaches.

A Hansom cab, designed in 1834 by Yorkshire architect Joseph Hansom (1803–82).

Omnibuses were soon not only carrying passengers from the town out to its suburbs and outlying districts, but also on routes that criss-crossed the town. However, to be economic, buses were soon carrying anything between twenty and fifty or more passengers, on an upper and lower deck. Triple-decked buses were experimented with but, as passengers did not feel very safe in them (with good cause) these were soon discontinued.

This meant that, once again, horses were required to pull dead weights that stopped and started with great frequency. Each time they did the animals then needed great strength

An omnibus at Mann Island in Liverpool. (Discover Liverpool Library)

to get the vehicle and its often full-capacity load moving once more. Because of this each omnibus needed to change its horses up to eleven times a day to maintain a service, and to ensure that the animals were not worked to death.

Despite the increase in suburban railway routes in the later nineteenth century, these did not generally carry people across conurbations, so horse-drawn local transport was still required. In fact, across Britain the number of horses pulling local omnibuses increased from 103,000 in 1851 to 464,000 by 1901. Even so, buses were only for the middle classes, as working people still usually walked everywhere and often for several miles. Nevertheless, demand for urban public transport continued to grow, especially across rapidly expanding Liverpool and Merseyside.

Of course, the number of passengers on a bus was limited by the capability of even a pair of horses to pull each vehicle. A more efficient system had to be introduced.

One way of increasing passenger capacity was to run buses along iron rails set into the road, so as not to impede other vehicles or their horses. The railways had shown that friction was reduced by pulling a carriage on rails. This also made it easier for a pair of horses to pull a heavier passenger load, thereby increasing profits; and it was in Birkenhead that the first street tramway in Europe was established.

This was opened on 30 August 1860 by an American entrepreneur with the appropriate name of George Francis Train (1829–1904). The global exploits of this amazing character would fill a separate book: suffice it to say that the French Novelist Jules Verne (1828–1905) based the character 'Phileas Fogg', in his story *Around the World in Eighty Days*, entirely on Train.

The horse-drawn tram system in Birkenhead proved so successful that it was expanded to include Wallasey. Soon Southport, St Helens, and Warrington also had tram systems. Before long other towns and cities across Britain had horse-drawn tram systems for their citizens, as did towns in Europe and America. Indeed, trams were soon being built for export at Birkenhead.

George Francis Train (1829–1905), tramway pioneer. (Discover Liverpool Library)

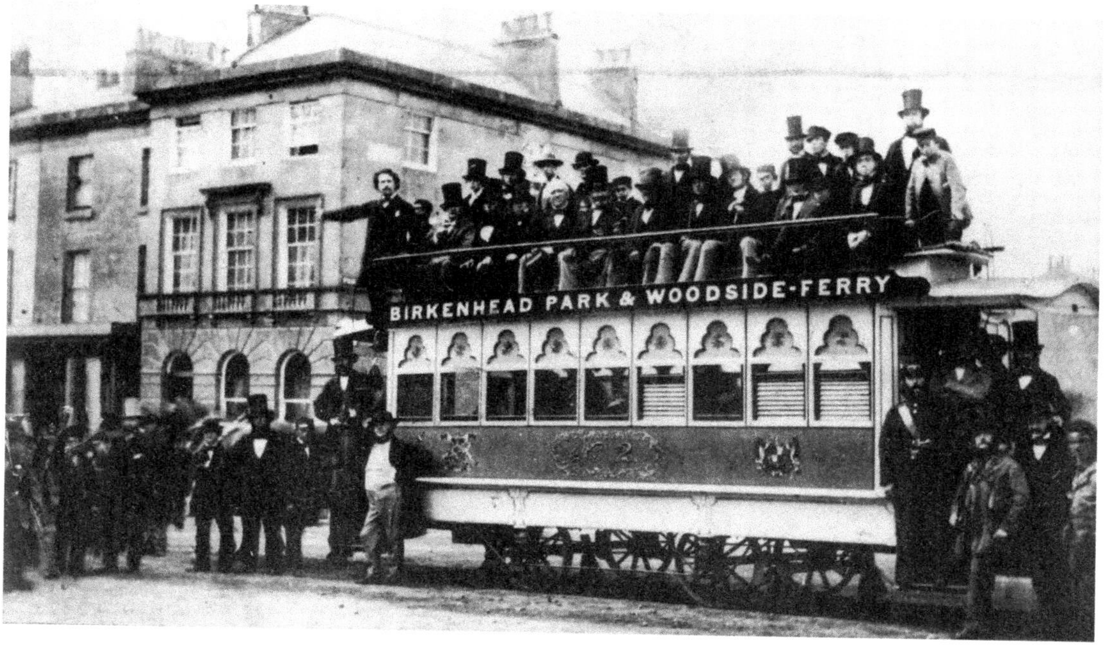


George Train with the very first tram in Birkenhead, in 1898. (Discover Liverpool Library)

By 1869, the first horse-drawn trams were operating in Liverpool. The town had, in 1868, been the first British town to obtain an Act of Parliament to run a comprehensive tram service. In 1914, it was also the first to have central reservations separating trams and their tracks from other forms of road transport.

Initially owned and run by private companies, trams first operated on a circular route around the city centre. Soon, other lines carried passengers to Walton and Dingle, on tracks covering approximately 60 miles. On the Dingle line alone sixteen cars, each drawn by three horses, carried an average of 7,000 passengers each day.

In 1876, several competing private tram and omnibus companies merged to form the Liverpool United Tramways and Omnibus Company. This was then operating with 2,894 horses and 207 tramcars in the city. In that same year though, this, and most remaining private tram companies in the Liverpool area, was taken over by Liverpool Corporation.

In 1883, it was recognised that horse tramways were, in fact, more complicated to maintain and more expensive to operate and, from that same year, no more tram tracks were laid. Indeed, between 1898 and 1902, the city's tram network was electrified, and in that year the last horse tram ran in Liverpool.

The tram system on Wirral had already been electrified in 1901, and so now Merseyside horses were finally relieved of this particular labour. Nevertheless, this was only as far as mass public road passenger transport systems were concerned, and horses still hauled goods and commodities along roads and canals.

Horse-drawn omnibuses began to be replaced by mechanical vehicles soon after the First World War.

# 5. Strength, Grace, and Service

## The Carters and The Community

Horses served mankind in commerce and industry too, including, sadly, being forced to work down coal mines. Before the invention of steam engines and steam locomotion, haulage of coal both above and below ground was carried out by women, children and, only occasionally, by ponies. This was because these people were small enough to fit in the pit passageways. Men were too valuable to use in this way as they were labouring continuously at the coalface. The first recorded use of ponies underground in British mines was in the Durham coalfield in 1750.

However, this changed following a newspaper article published in 1838, which reported that twenty-six children had drowned when the Huskar Colliery in South Yorkshire had flooded. This also revealed to the wider public that not only children but also women were being employed in this way, and there followed a public outcry against the practice. This resulted in the passing of the Mines and Collieries Act 1842, which banned women, as well as girls and boys under the age of ten (later amended to thirteen), from working underground.

Nevertheless, the work had to be carried out, so it was from this time that the use of horses and ponies in mines increased significantly. Coal was mined locally at Prescot, St Helens, Huyton, Haydock, and Skelmersdale. Ponies worked down Merseyside mines including those at Parkgate and Neston on Wirral, and at Cronton Colliery near Widnes.

Pit ponies worked long hours in almost total darkness. (Discover Liverpool Library)

As the twentieth century unfolded however, and although much of the work down mines could now be done mechanically, even by 1913 there were still 70,000 ponies toiling underground alongside British miners. As late as 1984, fifty-five ponies were still in use with the National Coal Board, mainly in the Ellington pit in Northumberland. The last British pit pony was probably Robbie, who retired from the Pant y Gasseg mine, near Pontypool, in May 1999.

As we have seen, and before the invention and development of the internal combustion engine at the end of the Victorian era, horses had been the only reliable, effective form of motive power that was widely and readily available.

For a time, they not only drew trams and omnibuses, but they also raced through the streets pulling fire engines across Liverpool, as well as in other towns around Merseyside. In the city these animals were so well trained that, when the fire bells rang, they automatically lined up in front of their engines as soon as they were released from their stalls. Their harnesses were suspended from the ceiling and were lowered into place on each horse. Apparently, this took only a matter of three or four minutes before they were ready to leave for the fire.

In 1880, the president of the Liverpool Medical Institution suggested a horse-drawn ambulance for the city. In 1884, this new service was created and based at the Liverpool Northern Hospital. This stood on Great Howard Street from 1834 to 1978 and was where the horses were stabled. This was the first such service in Britain.

Despite the growth of railways throughout the later nineteenth century, the increase in the amount of horse-drawn passenger traffic on the roads was matched by an increase in

Horse-drawn Wirral fire engine and crew. (Discover Liverpool Library)

goods traffic, which was also all horse-drawn. Around 161,000 horses were pulling freight vehicles in Britain by 1851. By 1891, this had increased to 500,000; by 1901 to 702,000; and by 1911 to 832,000.

Liverpool had the reputation for producing and utilising the biggest, strongest, and most loyal, steadfast, and resolute carthorses in Britain. They were well cared for and produced prodigious quantities of manure. Indeed, a survey of 1893 estimated that Liverpool had up to 16,000 horses employed in haulage, and that each horse produced 4 tons of droppings a year. As a point of information, horses pass a large amount of urine with their more solid droppings. This makes horse manure particularly acrid and offensive, especially if it is allowed to mature for more than a few hours, when it heats up and steams as it rots!

This was the case with the manure on Merseyside in particular, where it was simply piled up on almost every street corner, especially in the towns and larger communities in the region, particularly in Liverpool. Here, and well into the twentieth century, women and young children were employed by the Corporation as 'crossing sweepers'. Their job was to brush into these piles all the loose horse droppings from the sections of roadways where pedestrians generally walked or crossed. The stench in the city streets must have been appalling – until one got used to it, I suppose!

The piles or 'muck middens' were eventually taken away by other carters, to be mixed with old straw from many stables in the town, and then loaded onto canal barges. These then carried their smelly cargo along the canals, especially the Leeds–Liverpool, to the farming communities surrounding Liverpool. It was also carried on ferry boats across the Mersey, to be spread on the farmlands across Wirral. The crops this produced fed the horses and the people in return – the circle of life!

Crossing sweepers trying to keep some parts of the roads clear of manure. (Discover Liverpool Library)

This also explains why one can still see iron boot scrapers on the doorsteps of eighteenth- and nineteenth-century buildings, particularly in the days before roads were tarred or cobbled or had pavements. These were to enable householders and their guests to scrape off the horse manure (and dog droppings and mud!) that they inevitably accumulated on their footwear, and so not tread it into their houses. However, in the days of long dresses that dragged along the floor, these too had hems caked in excrement!

Upper- and middle-class women were slaves to the convention of never showing ankle or leg under any circumstances. They hitched up their long dresses whilst out walking on the busy streets and changed out of them as soon as they arrived home. They then expected their maids and servants to clean off any muck that might have accumulated on their hems.

Working-class women had little difficulty dealing with this issue as they simply wore their hems just above the ankle, or they had special street shoes and boots with elevated or platform soles. Many poorer people of course, especially children, could only afford to go barefoot. Therefore, the amount of filth on their feet and between their toes was paralleled by the squalor of the rest of their lives and domestic circumstances anyway, so was not really a consideration!

To enable horses drawing carts, carriages, and larger public transport vehicles to gain and sustain traction on the often steep streets and roadways of Liverpool, as well as on the quaysides and dockyards, a special form of road surface was employed: cobblestones. These are round or rectangular stones about 4 to 6 inches across, with either flat or rounded tops. They were often deliberately laid in uneven ranks to provide increased purchase.

Cobbles were first used by the Romans, but then fell out of use in Britain until the fifteenth and sixteenth centuries, when they made a limited return. By the nineteenth century, Liverpool Corporation and The Mersey Docks and Harbour Company laid and maintained millions of cobblestones. These were for horseshoes that saw so much heavy work that they had to be changed every three to six weeks.

The use of horsepower in the movement of goods and commodities reached a peak during the early 1900s. This was when more than 20,000 horses were working on the streets and docks of the port, and in its suburbs. Of course, not everything always went smoothly for carters.

Carthorses were very well trained by their masters and generally obeyed single-word commands to change direction without the need for the carter to use the reins. A story from this time tells of a carter who had left his cart with its back end facing the edge of the wharf, at George's Dock near Mann Island. This was whilst he went into a nearby property to get his loading instructions. Unfortunately, a cantankerous parrot, in his cage, had been hung in the open window of the building. This bird had considerable language skills and a powerful voice. Suddenly, he decided to squawk out in a loud and audible voice, 'back – back – back' several times. The obedient horse immediately did as he had been ordered and proceeded to back up, right into the dock – cart and all. Whilst the cart was lost the horse was saved. I have no information about the fate of the parrot however!

Since the opening of Liverpool's first dock in 1715, and for over 250 years, horse-drawn carts and wagons crowded the streets, docks, wharves, warehouses, quays, and canalsides. They jostled for space amongst the throngs of dockers, labourers, tradespeople, sailors, and pedestrians, in the noise, dirt, soot, and smoke of the thriving metropolis.

*Left*: Carters on the cobbled dock road. (Discover Liverpool Library)

*Below*: Horse-drawn New Brighton laundry van. (Discover Liverpool Library)

They did so in declining but still significant numbers well into the 1950s and 1960s when, throughout my own childhood, I remember that most bread, milk, and coal deliveries were from horse-drawn floats. The rag-and-bone men, the corporation refuse wagons, the knife grinders, and chimney sweeps also serviced the public from horse-drawn vehicles. I recollect them all, and in my memories I can still hear the clip-clopping of the hooves;

the rattling of the carts, floats, and traps; the clanging of the metal-rimmed cartwheels; and the neighing and snorting of those glorious animals.

The relationship between a carter and his horse had to be a genuine partnership. A true, loving friendship was generally the rule between man and animal, and carters took pride in the well-being and appearance of their horses. This was demonstrated particularly in the annual horse parade which, by the mid-nineteenth century, had become an eagerly anticipated feature of civic life in Liverpool. On 1 May each year, hundreds of perfectly groomed horses, from the smallest ponies to the greatest shires and drays, paraded through streets lined with thousands of spectators, waving and cheering them on.

The animals were in their smartest rigs, most wearing highly polished horse brasses, coloured ribbons, and flower-bedecked collars. Many drew carts that had been freshly painted for the event, and that were also highly decorated and ornamented – as were many of the carters and their families who paraded with them. These processions were a public recognition of the crucial role that horses played in the life and economy of the community and were also a celebration of these exciting creatures.

The May Day parades also fêted the men, and many women, who worked these horses, and who fed, stabled, and cared for them. They also marked the roles played by the blacksmiths, farriers, harness-makers, and cart builders. These people had their own customs and traditions, as well as their own rules. Like the 'bargees' on the canals, the carters and their colleagues were a special sub-community and sub-culture within the wider population of Liverpool.

It was common for a very close bond to form between a carter and his horse. (Liverpool Record Office)

In the decades immediately following the Second World War (1939–45), the annual horse parades eventually stopped, especially as there were very few horses on the streets by then. However, on 10 May 1986, a 'Grand Horse Parade' was held around the city, to great public acclaim. It was hoped that this would become an annual event once again, but this was not to be. However, on 1 May 2010, a special ceremony took place. This was held at Mann Island, near Liverpool's Pier Head, in front of crowds of press, public, and civic dignitaries.

After the speeches, an 8-foot-high bronze sculpture of a magnificent carthorse was unveiled. Showing the animal ready to be harnessed to his next load, the artwork is named *Waiting*. This now stands as a fitting tribute to these special animals, and to how much Merseysiders depended on them for so many centuries.

Horses served to help man uphold law and order too. As early as 1836, the Liverpool City Police Force was established, and horses were needed to provide transport and power for this public service. At this time though, the police did not own or stable their own animals, as these were hired, as necessary, from local 'jobmasters'.

In 1881, Captain William Nott-Bower (1849–1939) was appointed as Head Constable of Liverpool, which was then the largest police force in Britain. He immediately began improving and modernising the force including, in 1886, the establishment of the Liverpool Police Mounted and Transport Department. Eight horses were bought later that year, and these became the first permanent provincial Mounted Police Section in the country.

The duties of the section included transport of prisoners, security patrols, and crowd control. Also, any urgent police messages that had to be sent were carried by mounted police officers. As well as helping to maintain law and order, they also provided control and escort services, as well as carrying out ceremonial duties.

The headquarters of the Mounted Section was originally at Hatton Garden, in Liverpool city centre. This was also the headquarters of the fire brigade, which was then part of the police force.

In October 1938, a new stables and central headquarters for the Mounted Section were opened at Greenhill Road, in the Allerton suburb of Liverpool. This remains their headquarters today and includes a large indoor riding school and training field.

As well as horses, for many years dogs have also played an important part in the policing of Merseyside. In fact, each area within the Merseyside Police Force has its own allocation of dogs and handlers. These work alongside other officers in the prevention and detecting of crime.

Records show that, from the end of the nineteenth century, police were occasionally using Airedale dogs to help patrol areas of the inner city and the docklands of Liverpool. However, it was not until 1953 that the Liverpool City Police Dog Section was officially established. This too is housed in the Allerton headquarters on Greenhill Road.

In the 1950s and 1960s, dog handlers generally patrolled on foot, mainly in the city centre. One of their principal responsibilities was the 'Bank Patrols' that mostly covered Castle Street, at the heart of Liverpool's banking district. Here, four officers with their dogs oversaw the movements of cash and other valuables. This form of police patrol ended in the early 1990s.

'Waiting' – The Liverpool Carters' Memorial, near Liverpool's Maritime Museum. (Discover Liverpool Library)

Merseyside police dogs are all highly trained, and many have special skills. These are particularly employed in the search for illegal drugs or explosives. There are currently seventy general-purpose dogs deployed in the force area, and sixteen of these have received specialised training to work with officers in the firearms department.

## The War Horses

Of course, horses served humanity in wartime as well as in times of peace. During the colonial wars waged by Britain as it increased the boundaries of its Empire, particularly during the eighteenth and nineteenth centuries, most battles featured the significant use of cavalry horses. This was chiefly the case at the start of a battle when the cavalry led the charge with lances forward and swords unsheathed. However, with the advent of the twentieth century, and the outbreak of the First World War (1914–18), this had to change almost overnight.

This was the world's first truly 'mechanised war', which depended almost entirely on the use of massed heavy artillery and mortars, and on armoured tanks and machine guns. The use of these turned what, in previous wars, would have been the battlefield into the vast, muddy, shell-pitted bog of 'No Man's Land'.

It soon became obvious that horses could not be used in such an environment, simply because they could not move easily across or around it. Also, the vulnerability of horses to modern weapons greatly reduced their value on the battlefield. Even so, the animals still played a significant role throughout the war and were used for reconnaissance and for carrying messengers. They also pulled artillery, ambulances, and supply wagons, and were used as pack animals to carry ammunition.

Packhorses carrying ammunition at Vimy Ridge during the First World War.

Despite the trench warfare in Europe, horses continued to take part in some battles and cavalry charges. These took place in other theatres of war where the fighting was more conventional. Cavalry and Mounted Camel units did have some success on Middle Eastern battlefronts, against a weaker and less technologically advanced enemy.

When the First World War had broken out Liverpool was chosen as a suitable port through which to import horses for use during hostilities. However, there was no appropriate site near Liverpool where the animals could be trained. Fortunately, Lord Lathom told the War Department it could use his estate at Lathom Park, free of charge. This was near Ormskirk, and more than 200,000 of the horses that went to war with the soldiers were trained at Lathom.

Horses arrived at Liverpool's docks from Ireland, and from places as far away as South America and South Africa. These were then shipped by rail from Princes Dock in the port, to Ormskirk and then on to Lathom Park, which had its own railway station. If any animals needed medical attention, they were treated at a veterinary hospital that had been set up at nearby Scarisbrick Hall.

Between August 1914 and November 1917, a total of 215,300 horses were brought to Lathom, and 210,800 of these were sent into active service. Some were stabled at reserve depots around Britain, whilst others went directly to the front to join cavalry regiments, or to be trained as work animals.

Conditions were just as bad for horses at the front as they were for the soldiers, and they too were wounded, maimed by artillery fire, or killed. They also suffered from infection and skin disorders and were injured by poison gas. Hundreds of thousands of horses died, and many more were treated at veterinary hospitals and sent back to the front. Whilst the presence of horses often raised morale amongst the fighting men, they also contributed to disease and poor sanitation in camps, caused by their manure and rotting carcasses.

Undoubtedly, thousands of horses gave loyal and devoted service during Britain's wars (not that they had much alternative), and there are many memorials to individual animals across Europe and Britain. This includes one near Higher Road in Halewood, on the southern edge of Liverpool. This is dedicated to 'Blackie the War Horse'.

Born around 1905, Blackie served with the 275th Brigade Royal Field Artillery 'A' Battery – 55th West Lancashire Division – during the First World War. This was with his master, Lieutenant Leonard Comer Wall (b. 1896), who was from West Kirby on Wirral. Wall received a military commission and was posted to the Western Front in September 1915.

Whilst riding Blackie, Lieutenant Wall was killed in action on 9 June 1917, at Ypres in Belgium; he was only twenty years old. He was buried at Lijssenthoek Military Cemetery at Poperinge, in the Belgian province of West Flanders. Blackie received severe shrapnel injuries in the same incident, was treated, and then sent back to the front where he remained for the duration of the war. He bore his visible battle scars for the rest of his life.

After the war, Blackie was bought by Lieutenant Wall's mother, who then loaned him to the Territorial Riding School in Liverpool. In 1930, the horse was retired and stabled at the Horses' Rest in Halewood. He lived here very happily and was loved by local adults and children until his death, at the age of thirty-seven, in December 1942. Incidentally, for some years Blackie was the lead horse in Liverpool's annual May Day Horse Parade, along with another ex-war horse known as Billy. Blackie always wore his late master's medals in the parades.

Blackie now lies in the north-west corner of the western field fronting Higher Road and was buried with his master's medals. The grave is well maintained and marked by an engraved headstone. It is surrounded by a low, ornamental, white picket fence.

The Animals in War Memorial, in Hyde Park, London.

Other animals have provided special service to man as well as horses, including homing pigeons. These birds have long played an important role in war. Due to their homing ability, speed, and altitude, during both world wars pigeons were often used to carry messages back to their home coop behind the lines.

Another special service animal was a black male German shepherd dog named Jet (pedigree name Jet of Iada), who had been born in July 1942 at a house in Garth Drive, in the Liverpool suburb of Mossley Hill.

Jet had been bred by Mrs Babcock-Cleaver and, as this was at the height of the Second World War, he was specially trained in anti-sabotage work. However, this was during the time of the massive, prolonged, Nazi bombing raids across Britain (and especially Liverpool), so he was also trained to search for people trapped in the rubble of bombed buildings. In all he assisted in rescuing 150 people.

In peacetime, support dogs for the blind and partially sighted are now a fact of everyday life. The first of these to be specially trained as guide dogs were Judy, Flash, Folly and Meta, and these were also German shepherds. In 1931, the dogs were bred and trained in Wallasey on Wirral by Muriel Crooke (1901–75) and Rosamund Bond (dates unknown). Three years after this a national charity, The Guide Dogs for the Blind Association, was formed, and this continues today, now known simply as Guide Dogs. Incidentally, the charity's website says that, 'The first known example of a special relationship between a dog and a blind person was depicted in a first-century AD mural in the ruins of Roman Herculaneum.'

Dogs are also specifically selected and specially trained to assist deaf and hearing-impaired people. They do so by alerting their owners to important sounds, such as doorbells, smoke alarms, ringing telephones, or alarm clocks. They may also work outside the home, alerting their owners to potentially risky or threatening sounds, including sirens, forklifts, reversing vehicles, and to people calling their owner's name. Like guide dogs for the blind, these animals can also liberate their owners, and provide much-needed love and companionship.

Jet of Iada, the heroic rescue dog of the Second World War, at work.

# 6. The Animal Kingdom on Display

By now it is clear that royalty and the aristocracy have featured significantly in the history of the relationship between man and animal on Merseyside. This remains the case as the story continues, especially when we now look at how animals were captured, contained, and put on display for the entertainment of a largely ignorant public.

A number of kings and queens throughout British history have kept exotic and wild animals for their own amusement. Also, dancing bears, performing monkeys, and the like were touted around medieval markets and more modern fairs and travelling shows, first for the peasantry and then later for the working classes.

By the late nineteenth century, fixed zoos for the public were becoming a feature of urban life. In the early twentieth century these had evolved into carefully planned and laid-out, beautifully landscaped 'zoological gardens'. However, the first such menagerie in this region was built for the private edification and research of yet another member of Liverpool's aristocratic Stanley family.

## The Knowsley Ark and the Great 'Aviary'

As we have seen, many Earls of Derby have been unique, in one form or another, but perhaps none more so than Edward Smith-Stanley, the 13th Earl of Derby KG. He succeeded to the title in 1834, at the late age of fifty-nine. Lord Derby's particular distinction was his absolute passion for his menagerie and remarkable natural history collection at Knowsley, together with his studies and research into the natural world.

Edward, 13th Earl of Derby. (Discover Liverpool Library)

An outgoing and gregarious character, Edward had a wide circle of friends who all respected him for his kindness, generosity, charm, and intelligence. He began his interest in natural history as a young man with the study of birds. Possibly from as early as 1800, at the age of twenty-five, he was buying live specimens for his purpose-built aviary at Knowsley, as well as for the aviary that he kept in the family's London house, in Grosvenor Square. He also kept caterpillars and made extensive notes on their activities!

At the same time, Edward was increasing his collection of museum specimens that included drawings, eggs, and bird skins, which he bought from dealers in London. Most of these specimens were mounted and arranged in glass cabinets, according to species, but he also had many specially constructed chests of drawers. In these he kept his collection of animal skins and other animal samples.

As his reputation as a collector grew, ship's captains sold him live animals as well as other specimens that they had brought back to Liverpool from overseas. Lord Derby's collection was truly extensive. At its peak it totalled 1,272 birds and 345 mammals. These were all live specimens and represented ninety-four species of animals and 318 species of birds. In due course his collection also included reptiles and even exotic fish.

This was in addition to his collection of stuffed birds and other natural history specimens, which he kept in a private museum. This took up an extensive suite of rooms on the first floor of Knowsley Hall. From about 1813, Edward also employed a taxidermist named John Sherlock. This meant that even animals that died could be preserved, mounted, and displayed about Knowsley Hall and his other properties, which they were in some profusion.

Knowsley Hall in the nineteenth century.

By 1830, Lord Derby's collection of live birds had increased considerably. On what was known as the Brew House Pond at Knowsley Park he had established colonies of wildfowl and an aviary, where he kept game birds, songbirds, and varieties of pigeons. The aviary also had a heated area called 'The Stoves'. In this were kept all the foreign birds that needed a warmer climate. These included orioles, parrots, toucans, and macaws. Maintaining his considerable exotic menagerie cost him around £10,000 a year. This was a massive amount for the time and the equivalent of £1,150,800 today.

Even though his live animals included hundreds of mammals, he could not bring himself to use the term 'menagerie'. He felt this was 'altogether foreign', and too commonplace and coarse a description for his endeavour, so he always referred to his collection as his 'Aviary'. Lord Derby's zoological garden occupied around 100 acres of land and water in total. However, this took up only a relatively small proportion of his huge estate at Knowsley.

To develop his collection, and the facilities needed to service it, he employed 400 labourers, plus around fifty horse-drawn wagons to carry supplies and removed earth, and he set them to extending the space and accommodation for his animals. Earl Edward's workers now laid out a broad carriage drive around a whole new area made up of sizeable enclosed paddocks with fences.

Each one of these contained a spacious building in which to house his larger creatures, such as the ostriches, antelopes, or zebras, as well as large units for waterfowl. He also set his labourers to laying out a network of service roads and pathways to interconnect these, and the storage areas and outbuildings that he also built to store food, fodder, tools, and equipment.

The Earl avoided keeping the larger cats (presumably for reasons of safety) and the higher primates, but his collection of live animals was eclectic indeed. It soon included deer, kiwi, anoa (a small and very rare water buffalo from Sulawesi), ordinary chickens and domestic cattle, game birds, and guans and parrots.

Edward Lear's drawing of a Stanley crane.

There were gannets, a skua from the Orkneys, a Carolina parakeet (a species now extinct), foreign squirrels, and field mice. He also had brush turkeys, wapiti deer (from North America), barbary deer (from North Africa), and hog and sambar deer (from India), as well as alpacas and llamas.

There were also eland, antelope, various ruminants, a flightless swamp hen from Lord Howe Island (off Australia), a Himalayan mountain quail and a paradise parrot (both species eventually became extinct), a variety of species of duck, a boa constrictor, and a long-tailed hopping mouse.

Earl Edward's animals were not kept as a zoo, and the public were never allowed to come onto the estate to look at them – although Lord Derby always delighted in showing them to his friends, and to guests staying at Knowsley Hall.

A few years ago, I was commissioned by the 19th Earl to write a new history of his family. In my research for this I was gratified to discover that, even by the standards of the time, the 13th Earl appears to have genuinely cared for his animals and birds. Edward Smith-Stanley did not simply regard them as specimens but as fellow creatures. They were well-fed and, for the Victorian era, their health and hygiene were carefully maintained.

This remarkable man died at Knowsley Hall on 30 June 1851. He was buried in the Derby Chapel at Ormskirk Parish Church. His coffin was made from one of his favourite oak trees from the Knowsley estate, and his funeral procession was over a mile long.

The Earl's son, who became the 14th Earl of Derby and British Prime Minister four times, had always hated his father's animals and birds. Fortunately, and to prevent his son from simply destroying them, Edward Smith-Stanley, in his will, bequeathed Queen Victoria first choice from his live animals. She decided on a pair of Impeyan pheasants.

The Zoological Society had second choice, and they selected a pair of eland antelopes. The Earl left large numbers of live animals to Regent's Park Zoo, in London. Some also went to the Liverpool Zoological Gardens that then occupied a site on West Derby Road near Sheil Park, and about which we shall hear more of next. Other animals were bequeathed to private collectors in Britain and overseas.

The Corporation of Liverpool had already agreed to accept the bulk of the museum specimens, which comprised around 20,000 eggs, as well as his large collection of stuffed animals, which included mammals, fishes, and birds. This collection formed the basis of the first public Museum of Liverpool, which was housed in a complex of new buildings on William Brown Street in the town, and originally named The Derby Museum.

The 14th Earl swept away almost all the now empty animal paddocks, compounds, cages, and buildings, and he re-landscaped the estate to remove most traces of them. The lakes remain, as do the now defunct and empty home and workshop of his father's taxidermist!

## The Lion in the Wheelbarrow & The Death of Rajah

Merseysiders loved their zoos, especially Liverpudlians, and the city itself had at least nine zoos between the early 1800s and the late 1930s. On a map of Liverpool dating from 1836, zoos are shown at Pembroke Place near London Road, and at Boundary Place in Vauxhall, but my research has yielded no information about these. As well as a zoo in

Everton there was also Hilton's Menagerie, which opened on Lime Street in 1851. Here the paying public could see lions and other carnivorous animals, and a pair of polar bears.

However, the town's first public zoo was located between modern Boaler and Farnworth Streets, in the district of Liverpool now known as Sheil Park. This had been an area of open land, gravel pits, and dangerous ponds named 'Plumpton's Hollow', covering an area of around 10 acres.

Set in a vale and bounded on all sides by high, sheltering embankments, Plumpton's Hollow was bought, in 1831, by Thomas Atkins (1767–1848). He owned what was then reputed to be the largest travelling animal show in the country. However, he had come to Liverpool to settle with his animals. He spent a fortune acquiring and transforming the land into the very attractively landscaped and imaginatively laid-out 'Liverpool Zoological Gardens'.

This opened to great public excitement on 27 May 1833. He installed several attractions, including a small theatre that held around 600 people. There was also a dancing platform where popular bands of musicians entertained crowds of paying visitors. A special feature was a great lake around which a spectacular fireworks display was given every night.

With winding pathways across well-kept lawns and passing ranges of colourful flower beds, patrons could explore mazes, test their skills on an archery ground, visit the 'hydro-incubator' in which chickens were being 'continually hatched by steam', and see a full-scale replica of Shakespeare's house in Stratford-upon-Avon. To further entertain his paying public Atkins provided musical concerts in what he had named his 'Musical Temple', as well as breathtaking hot-air balloon ascents.

Of course, this was principally a zoo and there were many beasts and birds on display. These included caged lions and tigers, with free-roaming antelope. There were llamas and

Liverpool Zoological Gardens built in Plumpton's Hollow. (Discover Liverpool Library)

zebras, and many other animals that had never been seen alive by the people of Liverpool, so they were a sensation. This included a 'liger', which is a cross between a lion and a tiger.

By 1837, also on display were buffalo, coatis, hyenas, jackals, lynx, a mountain cat, opossum, ocelots, pumas, and leopards. Visitors could also see a cheetah, which was said to be the only one in England at that time. Added to this were a variety of reptiles and monkeys, as well as squirrels, tortoises, a porcupine, otters, polar bears, and an Indian rhinoceros.

There was also a large bear pit with a tall, central pole. Here could be seen spectacled bears, a sloth bear, an American black bear, and European brown bears. One particularly large bear managed to escape from the pit and the zoo grounds, making his way on to nearby West Derby Road. The confused and terrified creature was pursued by crowds of people, and so he occasionally stopped his desperate dash to turn and confront them. Naturally, following the accepted behaviour of the time, this provided the people with an opportunity to pelt him with whatever came to hand, so off he charged again.

No one dared approach the animal except for William Mayman. He was the landlord of a nearby pub known as 'The Parrot'. Mayman already had a connection with Atkins' zoo because he had once been a keeper there. He had become a local hero when he rescued a young boy who was being mauled by, ironically, an escaped bear. The large financial reward he received for this act of courage had enabled him to buy the pub.

Now, the courageous publican approached the bear and tried to subdue him simply by strength; Mayman was a large and powerful individual. However, the bear did not want to come quietly and, in the process of eventually being subdued and captured, he tore a great gash in the landlord's arm. This was so bad that Mayman had to have his arm amputated.

Nevertheless, upon his recovery, Mayman saw a commercial opportunity. He re-licensed his pub as 'The Man and Bear' and commissioned a new pub sign showing him and the animal. This bore the text 'Mayman in the jaws of the bear'. This, for quite some time, increased the number of drinkers in the pub and Mayman became a celebrity. The pub stood on the corner of Hygeia Street and West Derby Road but has long since been demolished.

It cost a shilling to visit the gardens, which was quite expensive for the time, but people could also buy season tickets for a guinea, which gained them admission for a year. The zoo became so popular that visitors came in their thousands, and not just from Liverpool but from all over the region. To keep paying customers returning Atkins also booked the best performers and novelty acts of the day, including the great Charles Blondin (Jean Francois Gravelet, 1824–97).

Born in France, this exceptionally skilled tightrope-walker had become one of the best-known acrobats of all time, because of his always spectacular feats of dangerous aerial acrobatics. Blondin's greatest stunt to date had been in 1859, when he crossed Niagara Falls on a tightrope. He then did it again, only this time blindfolded, wheeling a barrow, twirling an umbrella, and carrying his manager on his back! This feat guaranteed him world fame, and he made a fortune by repeating it on high wires all over the world, especially in England.

Now he was one of Atkins' top-line celebrities at Plumpton's Hollow, where he made his first appearance, in 1860, to great local acclaim. However, when he returned to Liverpool

Charles Blondin in 1859. (Liverpool Athenaeum Library)

and the Zoological Gardens in 1863, he knew he would have to do something especially astounding to again win the approval of what was always a very tough audience – Liverpudlians had seen just about everything by this time!

So, to amaze his audience, Blondin crossed a high wire that had been stretched directly above the upturned heads and open mouths of hundreds of astounded Scousers. As they looked up aghast, along the tightrope the acrobat pushed a live male lion, strapped into a wheelbarrow. This incredible exhibition almost ended in disaster though because a guy rope became entangled around the barrow wheel. The tightrope walker, and his potentially ferocious companion, almost slipped and fell into the enormous crowd below. However, Blondin recovered his balance and continued his performance safely, to the roared approval of the spectators – if not the lion.

On the death of the zoo's founder and proprietor, Thomas Atkins, in 1848, the animals, the gardens, and all its attractions were inherited by his widow and two of his sons, John and E. Atkins, and they continued to operate it.

One of their most popular animals at this time was a huge elephant named Rajah, who was then thirty-five years old. All the visitors to the Liverpool Zoological Gardens loved Rajah, not just because he gave rides, but because he was renowned for his gentle personality. However, on the morning of 17 June 1848, he turned on his keeper.

It appeared that the zoo employee, Richard Howard, had been brushing out the animal's den and had ordered Rajah to move aside. The elephant had normally been very friendly with his keeper, and obedient, but this time he refused to obey Howard. The keeper now gave the elephant's tusk a sharp rap with his broom.

Elephants were always popular attractions in British zoos. (Discover Liverpool Library)

Rajah was infuriated by this and the noise of his angry growl filled the enclosure. With his body the elephant then forced his keeper up against the iron bars of the pen. The animal briefly brought his immense weight to bear on the keeper and, when he moved away again, Howard slumped to the ground. His body had been catastrophically crushed, sustaining many multiple and compound fractures.

The elephant then brought his foot down on his keeper's body, finally extinguishing what little life had been left in him. Other keepers now entered the pen, drove Rajah back, and Howard's body was taken away to await a formal inquest. He left behind a wife and two children.

The Atkins family decided that Rajah must be put to death, so they met with the Mayor of Liverpool and a stipendiary magistrate to seek advice. They confirmed that the animal should immediately be put down with a lethal cocktail of drugs. This poisonous compound comprised 2 ounces of prussic acid and 25 grains of aconite (wolf's bane), mixed with treacle and fed to the elephant on a bun.

Rajah swallowed the lot and, although he seemed to be in some discomfort, after a short while he recovered and simply wandered around his compound as if nothing had happened at all. The Mayor now put the Atkins brothers in touch with the commander of the local army barracks. This officer immediately despatched a company of more than thirty riflemen to the zoo to act as a firing squad.

The soldiers lined up in three ranks alongside Rajah in his cage and the front rank fired a volley of shots at him through the wide bars. Right away the second rank fired another volley, followed by the third rank. Rajah gave out great, deep bellows as his body received the bullets. He reared up on his hind legs with his trunk raised, and then fell dead.

The inquest into the death of Richard Howard was held the following day, when evidence showed that the keeper had previously ill treated the animal, and on the

The ruthless and brutal killing of Rajah. (Liverpool Athenaeum Library)

morning of his death the blow he had given Rajah's tusk had been quite savage. A rumour had been circulating that Rajah had gone mad, but this was proved to be entirely untrue. Whilst the elephant had indeed eaten the broom and its handle after killing the keeper, he was otherwise perfectly calm and quiet!

In summing up the evidence the Coroner said he was sad that the Atkins brothers should have so quickly ordered the elephant to be destroyed. He said it was clear that Rajah had killed his keeper because of the ill treatment that he had received. After only a brief deliberation the jury returned the following verdict: 'We are of the opinion that the deceased came by his death in consequence of having beaten the elephant unmercifully thereby causing the animal, in his fury, to kill him.' They also agreed with the Coroner that the elephant had been unnecessarily killed.

The following day the body of Rajah was dissected for disposal. This attracted around twenty surgeons and doctors as well as many fascinated, if ghoulish, spectators. However, upon first cutting open the belly of the great beast an appalling stench emanated from his bowels. This filled the animal's cage and forced just about everybody to move right away until the air cleared.

Then, three men began to remove the intestines and organs from inside the body by climbing inside and shovelling them out. However, the smell was still so overwhelming that one of the men almost immediately had to climb out again, whereupon he 'fainted from inhaling the noxious gasses'. According to newspaper reports, during the process of dissection not one of the rifle balls fired at the elephant was ever found in his body or entrails.

Rajah's remains were then boiled to remove his flesh. Next, all his bones, including his great skull and tusks, were piled up and put on display. Visitors paid extra to look at them. The Atkins family were not people to pass up a money-making opportunity, especially as the living elephant had been valued at £1,000 (almost £120,000). So, they reassembled the skeleton and mounted this in the centre of the gardens. This now attracted even more paying visitors to the zoo.

However, in 1859, the Liverpool Zoological Gardens was sold to a group of private investors but, in 1863, the company went bankrupt. This was despite the appearance of Blondin with the lion! The once popular and remarkable zoo was closed in 1866. It is believed that most of the remaining animals were bought by Belle Vue Zoo in Manchester.

Nothing remains of Plumpton's Hollow or of Thomas Atkins' renowned zoo and gardens. The area is now a large, modern housing estate, and the only claim to fame it has today is that here can be found George Harrison Close, Paul McCartney Way, Ringo Starr Drive, and John Lennon Drive.

## Pongo the Man Monkey & Eastham Bear Pit

Another popular zoo was named the 'Liverpool Zoological Park and Gardens'. This opened on Rice Lane in Walton, at the north end of the city, in the summer of 1884. Covering 30 acres, it purportedly cost £200,000 (£25,000,000) to create, landscape, and stock with animals. Amongst many creatures on display, some of which, typically for the time, could roam freely, were exotic birds, small wildcats, African cattle, bears, and leopards.

In a large, half-timbered monkey house were numbers of apes and monkeys. One of these was the star attraction at the zoo and was advertised as 'Pongo the Man-Monkey: The Missing Link'. What type of ape he was is unclear, but he was large, agile, and according to reports, 'almost entirely human'. In fact, some visitors believed he was indeed a man wearing an elaborate monkey costume. This is unlikely and he was probably a chimpanzee, a gorilla, or a large orangutan. Whatever, or whoever, he was, his antics, acrobatics, and very human qualities regularly drew large crowds.

The pleasure gardens that formed a large area within the zoo were extremely attractive, with winding pathways around colourful flower beds, shrubberies, and wooded glades. A report on the opening of the zoo described a boating lake and a large tearoom built around a quadrangle planted with linden trees, 'to form a sylvan arcade for alfresco concerts'. The report continued, 'There is a spacious hall for concerts, dramatic and other performances,

Entrance to the Zoological Park at Walton. (Discover Liverpool Library)

public meetings, and use of the terpsichorean art.' It went on, 'All the highest points of the various structures will be illuminated by electricity.' Other attractions included a hotel, an elegant restaurant, a variety of shops, meeting rooms for 'learned societies', an alleged 6,000-year-old Inca mummy, and a carved Maori temple.

However, despite all these delights, and the daily firework displays, by late 1885 the zoo was losing money. It was sold off by auction, in March 1886, when it was bought for £20,000 (£2,600,000). It continued as a zoo but now on a much-reduced scale. Then, in 1887, it closed for good and was subsequently removed.

One of the long streets that run off Rice Lane, almost opposite the old zoo site, is Rawcliffe Road. A walk up this leads to the large Walton Cemetery, itself a historic location. In the grounds here can be found the excellent Rice Lane City Farm. So, the district's association with animals is still 'alive and well', if only on a much smaller scale!

People residing on Wirral, as well as visitors to this very picturesque peninsula, also had access to zoos and other forms of animal entertainment, but principally at Eastham Ferry Pleasure Gardens. In 1816, the very fast (for the times) steam paddle-driven passenger ferryboat *Princess Charlotte* was brought into service between Liverpool and the village of Eastham on the Wirral coast. This service was a lucrative source of income for its owner, Sir William Massey Stanley (1807–63), who also owned a large estate of land surrounding the ferry landing point.

In 1846, Sir William built the luxurious Eastham Ferry Hotel close to his ferry pier. However, the following year he sold the estate, ferry, and hotel to Richard Naylor (1814–99), a Liverpool merchant. The new owner decided to develop Eastham as public pleasure grounds to boost the fortunes of the ferry and his new property. He named this Eastham Ferry Pleasure Gardens.

Naylor built a fairground and planted extensive flower gardens, as well as rhododendron walks and ornamental trees. There were also fountains and secluded glades for private

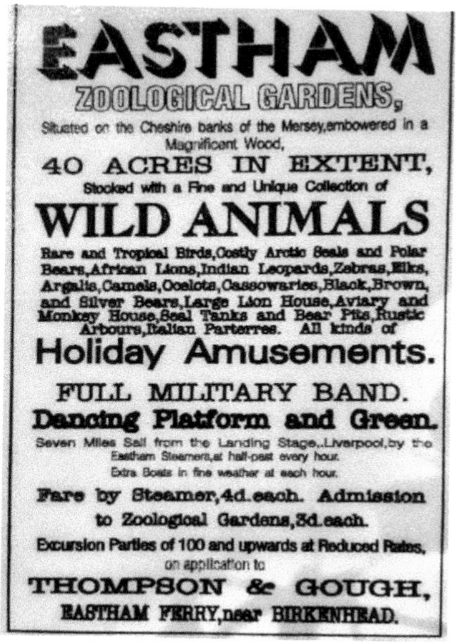


Eastham Pleasure Gardens Zoo sign. (Discover Liverpool Library)

canoodling and troth-plighting! He also provided band concerts, hobby horses, and a water chute. The investment paid off and the gardens became both popular and highly profitable. In 1874, a new iron pier was built for the ferry boats, and by this time Eastham had become known as the 'Richmond of the Mersey' (after the town by the Thames).

There was also a large menagerie in the Pleasure Gardens, with a bear pit, lions, tigers, antelopes, seals, a monkey house, and an aviary. Many people had never seen anything like this before. In fact, one middle-aged man was seen fleeing from the zoo screaming in terror at the sight of a large bear climbing the pole in the middle of its pit!

Interestingly, George Mottershead (1894–1978), who founded Chester Zoo in the 1930s, is said to have witnessed a keeper's cruelty to an elephant in the Ferry Gardens Zoo, which made him determined to ensure that the welfare of his own animals would be his top priority at his own new zoo.

As at the previously mentioned Liverpool Zoological Gardens, Charles Blondin appeared at Eastham too. This was at Easter in 1884, for a three-week engagement. Even though he was then sixty years old, the famous acrobat insisted on performing his death-defying feats, 75 feet above the ground, but this time without a lion!

Eastham attracted thousands of visitors from Liverpool and across the Wirral every week. In fact, during 1908 alone, 111,202 people visited the gardens. There was now also 'Fred Brook's Vaudeville & Circus Co.', a Pierrot Theatre, a large ballroom, sideshows, tearooms, an open-air stage, a looping roller coaster, and a boating lake – so there was something for everyone.

Unfortunately, the popularity of the Pleasure Gardens became their downfall, and they became somewhat seedy. Visitor numbers declined and, in 1925, the ferry service was discontinued. Now with very few visitors, in 1929 Eastham Ferry Pleasure Gardens were closed and in 1935 the ferry pier was dismantled.

The site of the old gardens is now Eastham Country Park. The Eastham Ferry Hotel still services visitors and, with pleasant walks through the woods, the excellent views across the river, and the fascinating remnants and relics from the old Ferry Gardens and Zoo, including the bear pit, means that this is still a popular destination for Merseysiders.

The bear pit at Eastham as it looks today. (Discover Liverpool Library)

The original Otterspool House (now demolished) where William Cross's family opened a zoo. (Discover Liverpool Library)

Other zoos operated in Liverpool, including one on the former estate and stately home of Otterspool House. This had been the property of a wealthy merchant, banker, and slave owner named John Moss (1782–1858). However, by the beginning of the twentieth century the estate and its grand mansion had passed out of the hands of the Moss family and were being leased by the Cross family. These were highly experienced animal importers and traders who had inherited the business from their renowned and highly successful father, William Cross (1840–1900). In 1916, Cross's sons, William Simpson Cross (1873–1920) and James Conrad Cross (1879–1952), opened a new zoo on the former Otterspool Estate, which they named Cross's Zoo Otterspool.

Sadly, conditions for the animals, staff, and the public were not of the highest standards at Otterspool, their being no health and safety executive or RSPCA in those days. This zoo was closed in 1930, when Liverpool Corporation bought the estate and began to convert it into the public parkland that is now known as Otterspool Park and Promenade. It was at this point that the zoo was transferred to the former Rosemont Estate, high on nearby Mossley Hill.

Confusingly also named the Liverpool Zoological Gardens, this was opened to the public in 1932, and was incompetently managed by Mr H. E. Rogers. Smaller than the Otterspool Zoo or any of its other predecessors, nevertheless the zoo became very popular with visitors. This was despite initial complaints from local residents who were very worried about public safety.

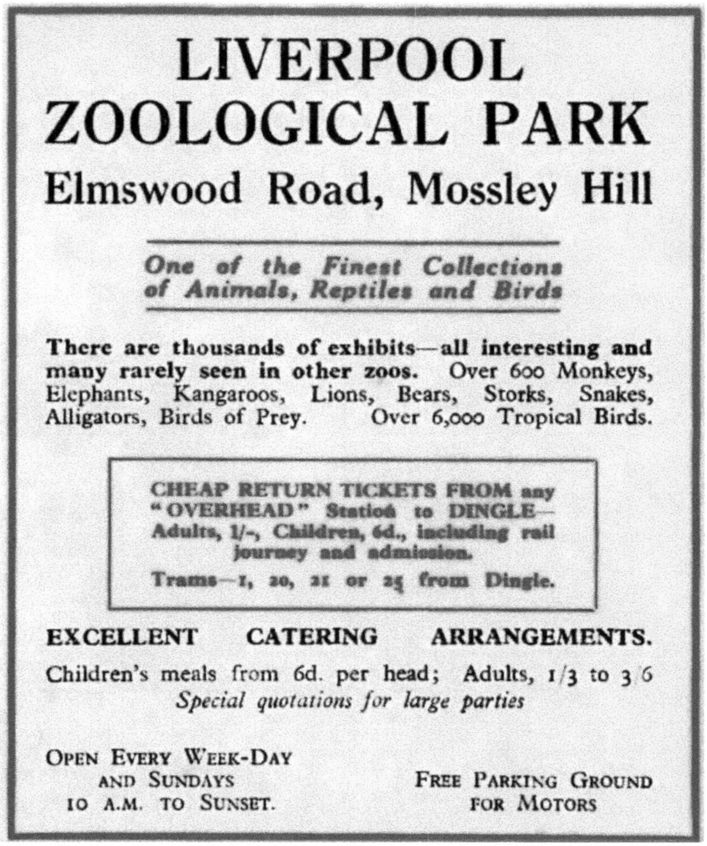


Poster for the Zoological Park on Mossley Hill. (Discover Liverpool Library)

These concerns were proved to be well-founded, as shall be seen later in this book, when I describe the incidents surrounding some of its animals, not least of all being the famous 'Mickey the Chimp'.

The most northerly zoo on Merseyside was Southport Zoo, in the seaside resort town of the same name. This was also the most recent of the region's zoos, opening in 1953 on a 6-acre site near the seafront and the 'Pleasureland' fairground. I remember this zoo well and, even as a small boy, I was always struck by how small it and all its cages and compounds were.

There were many protests by animal rights campaigners, and finally, in 2004, the local council refused to allow the owners to renew the lease. They gave the site to the fairground next door for their own expansion projects. Some of the animals were sold or given away, but the owners took many with them when they moved to Yorkshire. Here they opened a falconry and conservation centre, which has now also closed.

With the closure of Southport Zoo, Merseysiders saw the last of the many zoos and menageries that had featured in the history of their entertainment over the previous 200 years. Even so, this was not the last opportunity they would have to view wild animals in local captivity, as we shall see shortly.

# 7. Menageries on The Road

Itinerant performers and entertainers have travelled around British towns and villages since the earliest times, but especially after the Norman Conquest in 1066. As well as minstrels, mimes, and jugglers, animals including dancing bears, acrobatic dogs and monkeys, talking parrots, and other creatures were being shown to eager people who were otherwise starved of entertainment. The first troupes of performers began touring throughout the medieval period, and animals were always at the heart of their programmes.

However, the 'father' of what we would recognise as modern circus was a skilled horseback rider named Philip Astley (1742–1814). His performing career began in 1768, when he first toured Britain performing open-air acrobatics with his horse. This was so popular that he soon added other acrobats, tightrope walkers, jugglers, and a clown to his act. He performed his shows in a circular arena, which he called a 'circus'. He soon began giving these larger shows in available indoor spaces as well as under large canvass marquees. These became known as 'Big Top' tents.

Soon other performers were following Astley's lead, and families of entertainers began the circus tradition we know today. In the nineteenth century, 'Lord George Sanger's Circus' was one of Britain's largest touring circuses, and towns on Merseyside featured regularly on their itinerary. By 1858, Sanger's Circus advertised that it owned the largest stud of performing horses ever seen in the European continent, and they visited over 200 towns in a nine-month season, giving two shows a day. They also had over six lions and ten elephants in their show. Indeed, when the circus visited Birkenhead and Liverpool, in 1898, they also featured the skeleton of one of their previous performing pachyderms!

By the beginning of the twentieth century circuses had evolved to include increasingly theatrical and spectacular human performers, such as trapeze and high-wire acrobats, knife-throwers, and human cannonballs. However, animals were always the main attraction. Now, not only horses but camels, elephants and, of course, lions and tigers were being trained to perform for increasingly larger audiences.

This was also the time when circuses began putting their large stock of animals on display between shows and charging extra for the public to see them in their cages. These circus menageries proved to be very lucrative for the circus families, and often they bought extra animals simply for their travelling zoos.

At the turn of the nineteenth and twentieth centuries a particularly spectacular travelling show came to tour Britain from America. This was unlike anything that people had seen before, because it involved cowboys, Native American Indians, horses, and buffalo!

*Above left*: Teddy the Dancing Bear was well-known around Merseyside at the turn of the twentieth century. (Discover Liverpool Library)

*Above right*: Philip Astley, the 'Father' of modern circus. (Discover Liverpool Library)

## The Wild West Comes to Merseyside

In 1847, the great American Wild West legend Buffalo Bill was born in Iowa, USA. His real name was William Frederick Cody and, when little more than a boy, he became a rider for the pioneer mail delivery service, the Pony Express. In 1861, he began working for the US Army as an Indian scout, and he fought in the American Civil War from 1861 to 1865.

However, Cody earned his more familiar nickname when he became a hunter for the Kansas Pacific Railway in 1876. He was now tracking, shooting, and killing North American bison – more commonly known as buffalo – to provide meat for the workers building the great railway that was connecting the east and west coasts of the fledgling country.

Bill was an expert shot with a rifle and very skilled at his trade, so much so that he was said to have killed 4,280 buffalo in eighteen months. In fact, his record was forty-eight of the great animals killed in just fifty minutes. The problem was that he, and the riflemen he had working for him, almost completely wiped out the species and drove the Plains Indians into starvation. This was one of the causes of the Indian Wars in which Cody fought, gaining popular fame as a 'Wild West hero' for, in 1876, single-handedly killing and scalping Yellow Hair, the Cheyenne chief.

Cody became renowned across America and then around the world as the great 'Buffalo Bill' and, in 1884, he began to capitalise on his fame by creating 'Buffalo Bill's Wild West

Buffalo Bill and his Wild West Show came to Liverpool twice. (Discover Liverpool Library)

Show'. He toured the world with this extravagant entertainment, taking it to the greatest cities of the world which, of course, included Liverpool.

He first brought his show to the city from 6 to 18 July 1891, where it performed twice daily in Newsham Park – and what a show it was! The men and women of this great spectacular, with their animals and equipment, arrived at Knotty Ash station on Sunday 5 July, aboard a special train of seventy-two carriages.

These were carrying 200 performers, including cowboys, rough-riders, a unit of US cavalry, and Native American Indians, as well as 200 horses, dozens of covered pioneer wagons, and a herd of buffalo. They paraded their way through the suburbs of Liverpool to the park, attracting vast crowds of astonished onlookers en route.

In a huge, purpose-built outdoor arena paying audiences witnessed the roping and branding of cattle; the horsemanship skills of the rough-riders; and the recreation of a Sioux Indian attack on a wagon train, which featured the real-life Native American Indian chiefs Short Bull, Kicking Bear, and Long Wolf.

Thousands of people travelled across Merseyside every day, paying a shilling a time to see the show. Extra ferries had been laid on to carry spectators across the river. Special additional trams and omnibuses brought people from across the city and beyond, to shout in thrilled excitement as the one and only, authentic, actual Deadwood stagecoach was attacked by bandits.

Adults and children alike were amazed to see the world-famous sharpshooter Annie Oakley (1860–1926), known as 'Little Sure Shot', shoot the pip out of an ace of spades at 100 yards distance. But, to see the great man himself, Buffalo Bill, ride into the arena, leap down from his horse, and sweep off his hat in an impressive bow really brought the crowds to their feet.

Here he was in person, just as they had seen him in photographs in the newspapers, and in sketches in the 'penny dreadful' comics they had all been reading. With his long, flowing white hair; curling moustache and neatly trimmed goatee beard; in his white buckskins; fabulous boots with their engraved buffalo figures; and wearing his silver six-guns with their pearl handles, Buffalo Bill brought the Wild West to life in Liverpool.

At the end of the two-week run ¼ million people had seen the show and £20,000 had been taken, which is the equivalent of over £2½ million today. Bill was so happy with his profits that, in May 1903, he paid a return visit to the city. This time the Wild West Show took place in a massive, purpose-built Exhibition Arena on Edge Lane Drive. This stood where the Corporation Bus Sheds were later built, and where Wavertree Technology Park now stands.

The arena was 185 feet wide by 440 feet long and had tiers of seats on three sides. It had an accompanying exhibition of displays and attractions that covered 10 acres. These included a recreated Native American village and, of course, a menagerie where people could see the horses and buffalo at close quarters.

Nevertheless, and despite his worldwide fame and all the money he made, William Cody became bankrupt in 1915 and died in poverty in 1917, at the age of seventy. His body lay in state in Denver, Colorado, for just a day, but 25,000 people filed past his coffin to pay silent tribute to the great legend and showman.

The memory of his two visits to Liverpool, with his amazing and spectacular Wild West Show, lived long in the hearts and minds of Liverpool people, and we shall certainly never see the like of Buffalo Bill again.

Throughout the twentieth century, certainly until the 1970s, famous touring circuses in the region included Billy Smart, Bertram Mills, Gerry Cottle, and many more. These had

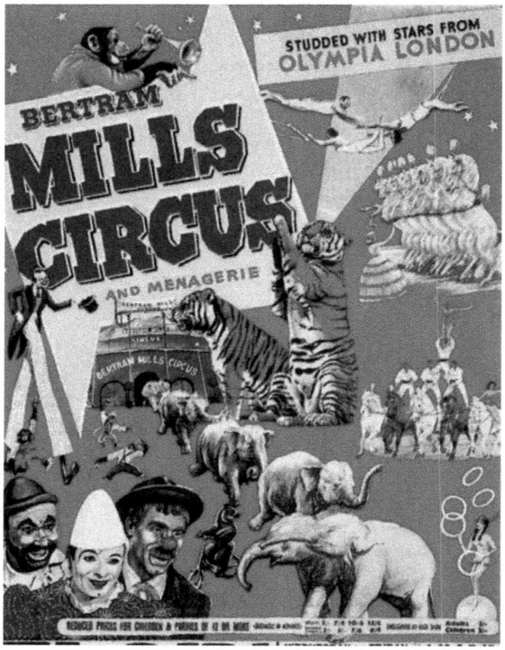


Poster for Bertram Mills Circus. (Discover Liverpool Library)

always drawn capacity crowds who delighted in the bareback horse riders; the parades of elephants, camels, and zebras; but especially in the lion and tiger tamers.

However, by the 1980s and 1990s, there was a considerable increase in awareness of animal rights, and a more empathetic understanding of the needs of all creatures, especially those in captivity. There were increasingly militant campaigns from animal welfare, anti-animal cruelty, and animal rights groups. Indeed, to attend an animal circus at that time audiences often had to run the gauntlet through lines of vocal protestors.

Public opinion soon sided with the campaigners, but legislation was slow to follow. The Animal Welfare Act 2006 was passed, and a licensing scheme for circuses was introduced in 2013, with a complete ban coming into effect only in 2020. In the meantime, though, and recognising that the weight of opinion was against them, circuses that included performing wild animals had virtually disappeared before the millennium. However, dogs and birds are still used as performers in circuses, and on stage and television.

Today, and whilst there are very few touring circuses, and these are certainly much smaller than they were even fifty years ago, these are much more enlightened. They still provide popular and thrilling entertainments as they travel the country, but now without the need to exploit animals.

Sometimes though, instead of animals travelling around the countryside to be on display, people drove around the animals instead.

## On Safari in Knowsley

During the middle decades of the twentieth century, the Chipperfield family were also well-known across the UK for their spectacular touring circuses. The 1950s and 1960s were the modern heyday for such shows, and the Big Top marquees of such circus dynasties appeared at open-air venues all over Merseyside.

However, as the 1970s approached, and to keep pace with changing public tastes, Jimmy Chipperfield (1912–90) knew he had to diversify to survive; and so did Edward John

The 18th Earl of Derby and a few of his rhinos. (Courtesy of the Earl of Derby)

Stanley (1918–94), the 18th Earl of Derby, on his Knowsley estate. The 'playboy' reputation of the Earl, in the media and entertainment world, encouraged the circus proprietor to approach him with the idea of opening a safari park at Knowsley.

Chipperfield's proposal to Derby was that paying visitors would sit in their cars and drive around a specially laid-out route through a large, cordoned-off section of Knowsley Park. They would pass large compounds and paddocks, and go through open but enclosed reserves, where they could see wild animals at close quarters. This would be a mix of thrill, spectacle, and novelty that Chipperfield felt would be both popular and profitable.

Lord Derby was soon convinced, especially as this was not a new idea. In fact, the Marquis of Bath had opened the first safari park outside Africa, in 1966, on his Longleat Estate in Wiltshire and it was making money, so why not one in the north of England too? The Earl was, in a way, reviving the menagerie or 'aviary' of his predecessor, the 13th Earl, but now in a quite different way and as a distinctive public entertainment.

A deal was struck. Chipperfield would source, provide, manage, and maintain the animals, and help design the safari park enclosures and layout. For his part, Lord Derby would provide the location and entrepreneurial expertise, and find the capital for the venture. In fact, this would be a £1 million operation so, to raise the necessary funds the Earl had to sell some works of art from his extensive collection.

The capital was raised; the driving route, enclosures, paddocks, and animal houses were built; storerooms, keeper's areas, and other resources and buildings were designed and constructed; as were the public and service roads. All the facilities needed for a major tourist destination were also built, including administration offices, ticket booths,

Knowsley Safari Park on opening day. (Courtesy of the Earl of Derby)

car-parking facilities, lavatories, souvenir shop, and a restaurant. This was a major project that demanded a high level of planning and delivery if it were to open on time and be successful. But all was not plain sailing.

As well as very precise planning permission being required, plus all the necessary legal permits for the importation, transportation, healthcare, and supervision of wild animals, the secure caging of them was a main priority. Liverpool and Knowsley Councils, as well as the local public and the press, needed to be reassured that when people returned home from work, or woke up on Sunday mornings, they would not find monkeys raiding their fridges, elephants trumpeting up and down their roads, or lions prowling around their gardens! Even so though, some animals did indeed escape their confines.

Fortunately, and despite subsequent local myths and bar room tales, none got outside the walls surrounding Knowsley Park. However, after a workman left an internal gate open, contractors had to use tractors to try and round up a wandering herd of wildebeest and return them to their paddock. A few giraffes were also found wandering around the estate, one of which got stuck in the mud on the edge of the lake, broke its leg, and had to be shot.

A postman calling at one of the lodge houses on the perimeter of the estate discovered a hippopotamus in the garden behind the house. A sea lion also made its way to the lake and was found making a home for itself under the boathouse. Then, a troop of apes broke out of their enclosure at night and made their way to the rear of Knowsley Hall. Here, they were attracted by the light coming through the windows of the servants' quarters on the ground floor, so they tried to break in, terrifying the female staff members in the process!

Obviously, with a venture of this sort, the safety and security of people and animals were of paramount importance. Serious lessons had to be learned therefore, when the lions tunnelled under the fence surrounding their enclosure to get access to the cheetah compound next door. Though extremely fast runners, these smaller cats had nowhere to run to, and so provided the lions with an enjoyable and unscheduled meal!

Following these incidents Lord Derby was determined to upgrade the level of professional management running his safari park and ensure that everything was perfect. This he did and, in July 1970, Knowsley Safari Park opened to great public acclaim and success.

Today, the 5-mile-long tourist driving route means that visitors pass alongside and through paddocks, enclosures, and open reserves covering an area of 550 acres. Happy and excited people, adults as well as children, can indeed see at close quarters a pack of cheetahs, prides of lions, herds of elephants, troops of monkeys, as well as giraffes, antelopes, tigers, and zebra. They can also get close to herds of camels and water buffalo grazing in large expanses of open pasture.

Amongst the most popular creatures of all though are the white rhinos. These large, formidable, and armour-plated animals add to the thrill and novelty value of the park and, over the years, they have drawn hundreds of thousands of tourists to Knowsley. Of course, this is a highly endangered species, and the breeding of these animals at the park is one of the main priorities of its current owner, Edward Richard William Stanley (b. 1962), the 19th Earl of Derby. He succeeded to the title in 1994 upon the death of his uncle, the 18th Earl.

White rhinos of Knowsley and a companion gnu (wildebeest)! (Courtesy of the Earl of Derby)

Indeed, conservation and preservation of all the species of animals at Knowsley is taken very seriously by Lord Derby, and by all his many staff at the park. The park, which celebrated its fifty-first anniversary in 2022, employs highly skilled and experienced conservation teams. These oversee the care and maintenance of the animals and their habitats and connect with communities and agencies across the world to protect biodiversity. With specialised breeding programmes they also help to preserve endangered species.

Because of this the safari park is an undoubted asset to the scientific credentials of Liverpool City Region. The park also remains a highly successful local tourist attraction and one of the most popular with national and international visitors alike.

# 8. Curious Tales of Curious Creatures

To close this history of animals on Merseyside, I will now tell a few curious stories of some special creatures, and how they have connected with people here. There are many more tales than I have space for, so this is just a small selection.

## Rodents, Amphibians, and Bugs

All over Cheshire and Lancashire, during the eighteenth and nineteenth centuries, many folk remedies and medicines were in common use. One that was very popular in rural communities and which was brought into rapidly growing Liverpool was a cure for children who wet the bed – mouse pie!

The recipe consisted of catching and killing mice and baking them into pastry. Alternatively, the tiny rodents could be dried out so that they were completely desiccated. Then the fur, flesh, and bones were ground into a powder. This could then either be baked into a pie or mixed with milk or water and drunk three times a day!

Caring mothers fed these remedies to their children and they were believed to be highly effective. In fact, these had been traditional remedies for centuries. Indeed, Dr Thomas Barnardo (1845–1905), who founded orphanages and a national charity that still bears his name, enthusiastically recommended mouse pie. However, it seems that the mere threat of being fed a mouse pie or mouse milkshake was enough to cure most children of their bed-wetting!

If you were suffering from certain infections during the Victorian and Edwardian eras, you could wait for the itinerant Toad Doctor to come around to your village. He especially frequented Cheshire and Wirral around this time.

This eccentric medic would cut off the hind legs of toads brought to him by his patients, and then put these into small bags, which he hung round the neck of those who suffered

from 'King's Evil' – otherwise known as scrofula – or from other swellings, rashes, or diseases of the skin. The bags were then worn continuously until the legs inside were entirely rotted. By this time, a total cure would have been effected.

Other remedies offered by the Toad Doctor included wrapping the right foot of a frog in a deer's skin and keeping it about your person to prevent gout. Or you could always cure sore eyes by catching a live frog and licking its eyes. Then, you held the frog against your own afflicted eye, in the hope that the frog would lick you back, when your cure would be instantaneous!

The doctor travelled around in his own pony and trap and charged seven shillings for each treatment – an entire week's wages for many of his patients. Whether or not they thought that this was value for money is not recorded.

On Low Hill in Liverpool, in the eighteenth century, once stood a large, well-appointed mansion house. This was surrounded by gardens and open fields. The great house was owned by a certain Mr Harrison and was directly across the road from the Coach and Horses coaching inn. This building is now the offices of an electronics company.

The main turnpike road ran past here, and one of Harrison's senior footmen, in full wig and livery, would stand in front of the inn waiting for coaches to arrive at this halt on their long journeys. As the passengers were disembarking, and before they went inside the Coach and Horses, the elegant servant invited all of them to enjoy a free hot meal, accompanied by ales and wines, inside Mr Harrison's luxurious home. Naturally, most people accepted this very generous offer.

They never met Mr Harrison, just his small army of staff who waited on them hand and foot. This was because Harrison was spying on them through a hole in the wall of his great dining room, with its massive dining table laid with silver cutlery, fine porcelain crockery, and crystal glasses.

The coach passengers were then served with bowls of thick, green soup. This was delicious but contained strange strips of white meat and little balls of something like tapioca. This was followed by large pies filled with another type of white meat and vegetables. Again, these were tasty, but they had very small bones in them. Sometimes

Rat's Castle around 1790. (Discover Liverpool Library)

Harrison's diners might find themselves picking clumps of hair from their teeth, or biting down on other balls of something that popped and then squelched in their mouths!

What Harrison's unsuspecting guests did not realise was that the eccentric and wealthy man liked to experiment with food: cooking rats, cats, and mice, complete with eyeballs and other, more peculiar animal body parts. He then secretly observed his unsuspecting guests as they ate, so that he could study their reactions as they realised what they were actually eating.

This was especially the case when it came to dessert, which often comprised delightful-looking tartlets, vol-au-vents, and dainty flans, into which Harrison had baked spiders, flies, bluebottles, and black beetles.

Because of this, local people soon named Harrison's mansion 'Rat's Castle', and coach travellers soon began to decline his invitations to lunch, afternoon tea, or supper!

## Cats Great and Small

The story of 'The Lion of Sleepers Hill' is told by author Tony Crowley in his 2012 book *Scouse: A Social and Cultural History*. It seems that on the morning of 4 February 1871, the McCardle Family Travelling Circus was making its way from Preston to Liverpool. Here, they were due to give a full show at the top of Anfield Hill, which is where Liverpool Football Club's Spion Kop would be built thirty years later.

They had got as far as Aintree where they made a stop to feed their animals. However, in the process their huge male lion escaped and ran off in the direction of Walton. As he stayed on the road he was easy, if exhausting, to follow all the way to Walton Hill. Then he loped down County Road and up Spellow Lane.

The great cat now made his way around the perimeter railings of Stanley Park, which had been opened the year before, but his trackers then lost sight of him. They decided to spread out and widen their search, because panic had really set in by now – they had to catch him before the animal ate anyone!

Surprised and terrified local pedestrians told them which way the lion had gone, round the back of the park and leading up the hill towards Anfield. Here, the searchers found

Let sleeping lions lie!

a track lined by gorse bushes and other shrubs and trees. Then, and to everybody's great surprise, they found their missing lion.

He had lain down on the track and fallen fast asleep against some gorse bushes. To their even greater relief there were no bloodstains around his mouth or claws! They were then able to throw a net over the recumbent animal and safely recapture him. They had brought his mobile cage with them, drawn by a very placid horse, and so they were able to get 'lost Leo' inside without trouble. That very night the lion gave a problem-free performance in the Big Top to everyone's great delight!

Up to this time this track and its hillside where the lion had been found had no formal name, but ever afterwards it has been known as Sleeper's Hill.

In the early evening of 27 June 1939, Chapman's Circus' Big Top tent had been pitched in the car park of Tranmere Rovers Football Club, on the outskirts of Birkenhead on Wirral. Whilst the show was in full swing with a full house, a fair-sized crowd of adults and children were outside the large canvass arena. They were standing close by and watching as the two tigers, Romeo and Bengal, were returning from their performance inside. The large animals were slowly making their way through a long, low, narrow, wire tunnel to their mobile cage in the car park. However, one of the circus hands was distracted for a few moments and did not notice that the tunnel had an unexpected gap in it.

The tigers simply walked through this and out into the car park as the crowd of spectators now quickly scattered! Fortunately, the 'big cats' did not give chase; in fact, Bengal wandered back through the open main entrance of the Big Top, which was still full of happy circus-goers.

Luckily, just as members of the audience saw the great beast lope into their midst and before a mass panic began, the huge tiger was quickly captured and returned to his cage. However, Romeo made his escape from the car park into adjacent Borough Road, and suddenly leapt through the hawthorn hedge in front of some of the houses, and into their front gardens!

Romeo recaptured and reunited with Bengal. (Courtesy of Liverpool Echo)

Romeo, now lay down in the front garden of house No. 749, was aroused when a police van arrived with its bells ringing. Circus hands turned up too with a travelling cage, inside which was Bengal. This was to lure the other tiger inside, but Romeo simply made his way across into the adjoining gardens.

When he reached No. 745, an animal trainer managed to coax the tiger into an open garage on the property. He quickly closed the doors on the animal as soon as it was safely inside. Looking through the window he could see that, fortunately, Romeo had immediately settled down and fallen asleep on the garage floor.

This gave the police time to position the open end of a now secure wire tunnel outside the garage door. This led directly to the tiger cage, which had been parked in the house driveway. One half of the garage double door was then opened, carefully and quietly, and the wire tunnel placed inside. The trainer now gently woke the softly slumbering animal, who roused himself and stood up. Romeo was then successfully coaxed into the tunnel and through to the cage, where he joined Bengal.

Both tigers were back in time for the evening performance, which went ahead as if nothing had happened!

Cats of a considerably smaller size, but very much older indeed, came to Liverpool in their thousands at the end of the nineteenth century. Late in 1888, a farmer digging in his land near Beni Hassan in Egypt discovered a mass burial tomb containing well over 100,000 mummified cats. More were excavated subsequently.

These had been ceremonially buried, over 4,000 years before, at a time when cats had been worshipped as the Goddess Bast (or Bastet). She was the goddess of love, passion, joy, women, and of pleasure. During that period she and all cats had been worshipped with great reverence – not so in the years immediately following the discovery though.

Topical cartoon in *Punch* magazine warning of ghostly cats on Merseyside farms. (Liverpool Athenaeum Library)

By this time farmers had found that mummified remains were a prime source of phosphates and made excellent fertiliser, so the excavators of the tomb quickly sold some to local farmers. However, in 1889, the bulk of the find was sold to a merchant in the Egyptian city of Alexandria. This entrepreneur recognised that there would be a profitable market for these in Britain, so he transported them to Liverpool in two steamships, *Pharos* and *Thebes*.

In the saleroom of Messrs Gordon and Co., in Rumford Street in the City, 19½ tons of whole and fragmented embalmed cats were auctioned. These were sold for £3, 13s. 9d per ton (£340). Their purchasers then ground up the mummies and spread them over fields in the region, as manure.

At a second auction the auctioneer used one of the cat's skulls as an auction hammer! Indeed, many skulls were sold off individually as souvenirs of the arrival of the mummies in Liverpool. In fact, a cartoon appeared in *Punch* magazine that month depicting a farmer confronted by hundreds of zombie mummified cats!

In all, 180,000 cats' bodies were shipped from Egypt to Liverpool, and were all sold on as fertiliser. A few of the mummies were salvaged though, and they are currently on display in the World Museum Liverpool.

## The Earl and the Pussycat

For the next story we once again return to the Stanley family who figure so prominently in the history of Merseyside. I previously described the aviary (menagerie) that the 13th Earl of Derby built and maintained on his estate at Knowsley Park. However, whilst still only the heir to the Derby title, in 1831, Edward Smith-Stanley was visiting Regent's Park Zoo in London.

Here he noticed a young man sketching the animals, whom he later discovered was only nineteen years old. Curious, he quietly moved over to where the artist was standing, deeply engrossed in his work. When Lord Stanley glanced over the young man's shoulder he was stunned by the detail, intricacy, and the accuracy of the illustration that he was producing.

Striking up a conversation with the youth, the wealthy aristocrat was even more impressed to discover who he was. The artist was Edward Lear (1812–88), and his reputation as a natural history artist was already becoming well-known: Lear's book of watercolour paintings of parrots was currently being published, in sections, to great critical acclaim. Lord Stanley immediately offered the artist a commission to come to Knowsley to sketch the animals in his private collection.

It was at this point that Lear himself realised who he was talking with: Lord Stanley's own reputation was just as well-known and respected. The young man readily agreed and was to spend the next five years living at Knowsley Hall. During this time, he produced the most exquisite watercolours of the animals and birds, particularly the more rare and exotic ones. The result of these labours is 108 original, colour paintings, of exceptional quality and vibrancy, which are kept at Knowsley Hall.

Edward Lear was a shy, retiring young man, but he had a natural ability to communicate with children. He was also a very gifted impromptu story-teller. At Knowsley there were lots of children; not just those of the 12th Earl and Lord Stanley, but some young cousins too. These all delighted in hearing the nonsense tales and rhymes that the young artist so eagerly invented and shared with them.

Edward Lear was a very talented young artist. (Discover Liverpool Library)

On one afternoon, Edward Lear was keeping some of the Stanley children entertained in Knowsley Hall, when they said to him,

'Is it true Mister Lear, that you can instantly create a rhyme about any object, without thinking about it?'

'Yes, children,' he replied. 'Indeed, that is so.'

The children eagerly looked around the large drawing room and there, mounted solemnly on a stand, on a dresser, was one of Lord Stanley's large, stuffed owls.

'Mister Lear,' they shouted out excitedly, pointing at the bird, 'tell us a rhyme about that creature!'

Edward Lear thought for only a few moments, and then began to recite,

> The Owl and the Pussy-cat went to sea in a beautiful pea green boat,
> They took some honey, and plenty of money, wrapped up in a five-pound note.
> The Owl looked up to the stars above, and sang, to a small guitar,
> 'O lovely Pussy! O Pussy my love, what a beautiful Pussy you are,
> You are! You are!
> What a beautiful Pussy you are!

The children were fascinated and delighted by this and by his many other verses, as well as by the amusing drawings he produced for them to illustrate his rhymes. Many subsequent generations of children, and their parents too, have been just as entertained by these.

Lear published his sketches of Lord Derby's animals in 1846, entitled *Gleanings from the Menagerie and Aviary at Knowsley Hall*, and this became renowned for its technical

*The Owl and the Pussycat* as drawn by a young Edward Lear at Knowsley Hall. (Discover Liverpool Library)

accuracy. In the same year he also published *A Book of Nonsense*, based on the sketches and verses that had amused the children at Knowsley Hall. I feel sure that the artist and poet would be extremely gratified if he could see how much popularity and respect his nonsense verses still command today – just as much as his paintings continue to do.

## Liverpool's 'King Kong'

In the 1930s, one of Liverpool's most popular zoos stood in grounds at the top of Mossley Hill; this was the City's third 'Liverpool Zoological Gardens'. This had been established by the Cross family when they moved from the Otterspool estate. One of the public's favourite creatures on display here was Mickey the Chimp.

Mickey was a cantankerous, moody, male chimpanzee who weighed 13 stone. He was bigger than a man and all muscle, and had an adventurous personality. Despite his often unpredictable nature, Mickey's keepers regularly allowed him to wander freely amongst the crowds in the zoo – standards of zoo-keeping were quite different then!

Perhaps predictably, Mickey often escaped from the zoo and, on one such bid for freedom, he jumped the 8-foot-high zoo wall into the adjacent road. Here, when a passing coal cart driver attempted to intercept him, he simply threw the smutty merchant across the road, followed by his coal shovel.

The ape then kissed a woman pedestrian who was walking down the road and who had greeted him by name – Mickey was a well-known and popular feature of the district. He then accompanied her some way down the road with his arm around her. When a contingent of police eventually arrived to apprehend him, Mickey simply wrenched the batons from the hands of each officer and calmly threw them away. He only 'came quietly' when offered an orange held out to him by another woman – Mickey the Chimp clearly had a 'thing' for the ladies!

Mickey was a continual source of entertainment for the paying public, especially when he played football, which he always really enjoyed. He even had his own favourite football. His party piece was to stand in goal whilst volunteer would-be strikers from amongst the visitors tried to score. They seldom did though because the huge Chimp was a highly skilled goalie.

Sadly though, more than one frustrated 'Dixie Dean' aimed directly at Mickey, deliberately trying to hurt and provoke him with the tough, leather-case football. Mickey

Advert for the Liverpool Zoo at Mossley Hill, showing 'Mickey the Chimp'. (Discover Liverpool Library)

would then throw the ball back at those who hurt him, much to the amusement of the crowd, but to the frustration and humiliation of the poor ape. One such nasty encounter with the public provoked Mickey into his fourth and final escape. This was on 24 March 1938, but this time the ape's actions whilst at large were not so benign.

He leapt the zoo wall and made his way into the playground of nearby Sudley Primary School. Here, the children were doing their PE exercises under the supervision of their teacher, Mr Gall. The brave teacher placed himself between the ape and the children to protect them, but was quite badly gashed in the neck and thigh by Mickey, who then hurled the twenty-four-year-old young man, unconscious, across the playground.

Within a few moments the teacher came round and saw that the chimp was still in the yard. Fortunately, Mickey then bounded over the schoolyard wall into the nearby road, and so the teacher and the children made it safely inside the school building.

Mickey then climbed onto the roof of 29 Lugard Road, where fifteen policemen, a lion tamer, a zookeeper, four police cars, a Black Maria, and a coal merchant all arrived to recapture him. Immediately the coal merchant tried to coax him down, but whether this was the tradesman from the previous encounter I have been unable to establish. Neither can I say how he intended to persuade the chimp to leave his roof. I presume he had some bananas to hand as I cannot imagine that half a cwt (hundredweight) of nutty slack would have done the trick!

Nevertheless, all attempts failed, and Mickey now began to tear slates from the roof and hurl them into the street. As he was now clearly dangerous, Mickey was shot and severely wounded in the throat by armed policemen who had arrived on the scene. He rolled off the roof and fell into the yard at the rear of the property. Witnesses watched as he crawled into a corner of the yard in great pain.

Whimpering and very weak, Mickey reached out for an old, scuffed, discarded football that was lying in the yard. This was just like the one he cherished at the zoo, and he gently pulled the ball towards him.

At this point, Major C. J. Bailey of the 38th Anti-Aircraft Battalion arrived from nearby Fulwood Army Barracks. He fired two shots at the pitiful ape, which at last ended Mickey's suffering and tragic life.

Coincidentally, and remarkably, just five years before Mickey's final escape from the zoo, a film had taken the cinemas by storm. *King Kong* was the tale of a great ape who is captured by an exploitative impresario. He is then humiliated by being put on display before an uncaring public.

Driven to escape by his mistreatment, the ape then rampages around the streets and ends up at the summit of a high building. Here, he is shot and killed. He falls to the ground as a pitiful remnant of what nature had intended him to be. The parallels between King Kong's story and Mickey's are remarkable.

Mickey's escape, plus other incidents at the zoo, finally forced the authorities to close it down later in 1938. But, not wanting to miss a financial opportunity, the zoo owners had Mickey stuffed and mounted, complete with his football. He was placed on display in the basement of Lewis's Department Store in Liverpool town centre, where people paid 6d a time to see the body of the famous great chimpanzee.

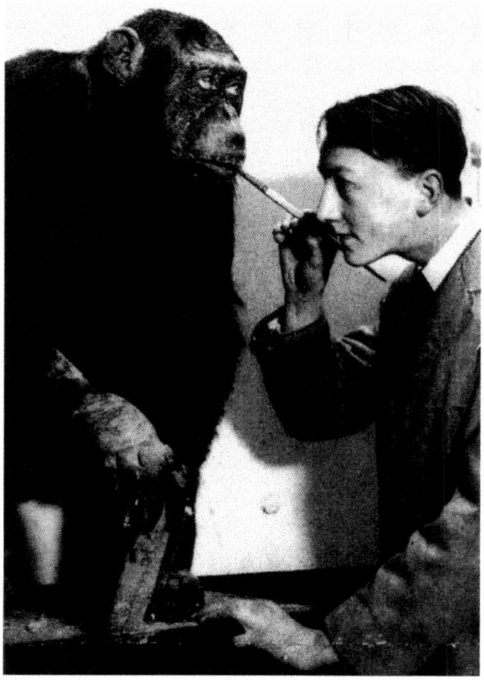

Mickey in 1938, being stuffed and mounted before going on display. (Discover Liverpool Library)

Finally, when Lewis's store was destroyed by Nazi bombing during the May Blitz of 1941, so was Mickey the Chimp, and Liverpool's own 'King Kong' was then gone forever.

My final story in this book is about a creature that is half myth and half real. Arguably, it is the most significant of all the animals to Merseysiders, and to Liverpudlians in particular.

## The Liver Bird

This special bird is the most iconic symbol of Liverpool and is recognised across the UK and around the world. Representations of it, in many styles and forms, can be seen everywhere throughout the city.

There is some confusion over the actual origin of the Liver Bird, and some scholars believe that its name is a corruption of 'Laver Bird', laver being the seaweed that it is always shown carrying in its long beak. This perhaps indicates a Welsh influence in the bird's name, as 'laver' is of Welsh origin, as in 'laver bread'. Liverpool and Merseyside have had connections to Wales for many centuries.

Also, cormorants once fed on the weed in the old creeks off the ancient River Mersey, and in the great tidal inlet or 'Pool' that gave the town its name. This is why it is often assumed that the Liver Bird image is based on this bird, which still can be seen feeding in and around the river. However, the more generally accepted origins are somewhat different.

In tribute to King John for founding Liverpool and granting its charter in 1207, the town decided to adopt the emblem of the monarch's house as its heraldic symbol. This was the image of the Eagle of St John the Evangelist. The eagle was drawn carrying foliage in its beak and, rather than this being seaweed, it was more likely to have originally been broom – the 'planta genista' of the Plantagenet family to which the King belonged.

The fortunes of the soon expanding town were assured, as its strategic advantages and commercial possibilities became apparent to subsequent monarchs and their aristocratic representatives. By the time of the English Civil Wars (1642–51), when, in 1644, Cavalier forces besieged and sacked Liverpool, the town seal was lost. In 1655, it was replaced by a new seal. However, because of the seeming ineptitude of the artist, the image looked more like a seagull than an eagle. Over time, and subsequent re-drawings, the bird came to be regarded as a cormorant.

In the Victorian era, during Liverpool's zenith, the city created a new official crest. On this, Neptune is shown on the one side supporting the emblem of the Liver Bird. He carries a trident in one hand and a banner bearing the Liverpool coat of arms in the other. The figure of Triton supports the other side of the emblem, and he holds a banner showing a sailing ship.

The most famous Liver Birds, of course, are the ones that proudly stand on the domes of the two clock towers of the Royal Liver Building. This equally famous building is one of Liverpool's 'Three Graces', which stand at the Pier Head, and it opened in 1911. The birds are each made from hammered copper plates that are bolted together on armatures of rolled steel. They each stand 18 feet high, the head of each bird is 3½ feet long, each leg has a circumference of 2 feet, and the wingspan is 12 feet across.

The massive birds need to be tied in place by steel cables because legend says that if they ever fly away then Liverpool would be doomed! They are also of different sexes with the female facing the river. She is waiting for the sailors to return home safely, following their long sea voyages. The male bird stands facing inland. He is watching to see when the pubs have opened!

These two greatest Liver Birds watch over the city and the river that made it great, in formidable yet benevolent guardianship. They also represent the perpetual relationship between the people and places of Merseyside, and the animal kingdom.

*Left*: King John's Crest – was this the source of the design for the Liver Bird? (Discover Liverpool Library)

*Below left*: Liverpool City coat of arms.

*Below right*: One of the two Liver Birds atop the Royal Liver Building. (Discover Liverpool Library)

# Conclusion

In this book I hope that I have proved just how crucial animals of all kinds have been in the history of Merseyside. Indeed, representations of them can be found, in many forms, around the region. They are seen in mosaics, carvings, reliefs, and paintings, and stand as castings and sculptures. They are also carved into doorways and lintels, and are found as gargoyles on churches.

In Liverpool there are four magnificent lion statues sitting on pedestals on St George's Plateau. Great American eagles are carved onto the corners of the Cunard and the Marks and Spencer buildings, with a smaller but impressive eagle on the former American Consulate Building on Paradise Street.

In the University of Liverpool precinct, on the Ashton Building, are two beautiful, sculpted, art deco sphinxes, and the frieze on the entablature encircling Liverpool Town Hall shows reliefs of elephants, camels, bears, crocodiles, great fishes, and other unidentifiable creatures. On the doors of the former Bank of Liverpool building on Water Street are two magnificent panther's heads. Their large, sharp fangs have been polished by thousands of people rubbing them for luck over the years.

Throughout the city are seven splendid equestrian statues and on the Paifong Arch in Chinatown there are 200 dragons, twelve of which are pregnant! These are all physical reminders of our relationship with animals, and of how much their lives are interwoven with our own.

Today we certainly treat animals far better than we did in previous centuries, and we do not exploit them to the same extent either. However, I do not feel that we respect them as we should. Nor do we place a true value on them as partners on the journey of life that we travel together.

The time is long overdue when we re-evaluate animals and our efforts to preserve, protect, support, and love them – all creatures great and small in Beastly Merseyside and beyond.

Ken Pye, 2022

# Bibliography

Belchem, J. (Ed.), *Liverpool 800* (Liverpool, 2006)

Brooke, Richard, *Liverpool As It Was 1775 to 1800* ( Re-pub. 2003, Liverpool Libraries and Information Services)

Chandler George, *Liverpool* (London: B T Batsford Ltd, 1957)

Chitty Gill, *The Changing Face of Liverpool, 1207-1727* (Liverpool: Merseyside Archaeological Society, 1981)

Clarke, Mike, *The Leeds and Liverpool Canal* (Lancaster: Carnegie Publishing, 1994)

Crick, M., *The March of Militant* (London: Faber, 1986)

Crowley, Tony, *Scouse: A Social and Cultural History* (Liverpool University Press, 2012)

Dutton, Roy, *Sixteen Decades in Wallasey* (Infodial, 2013)

Evans, R., *The Merseyside Objective One Programme: Exemplar of Coherent City-Regional Planning and Governance or Cautionary Tale?* European Planning Studies, 10(4), 495–517. (Liverpool: 2002)

F. A. Bailey, and R. Millington, *The Story of Liverpool* (Liverpool: Corporation of Liverpool, 1957)

Frost, D., & Phillips, R. (Eds), *Liverpool '81: Remembering the Toxteth Riots.* (Liverpool: Liverpool University Press, 2011)

Hand Charles, *Olde Liverpoole and Its Charter* (Liverpool: Hand & Co., 1907)

Heseltine, M., *Life in The Jungle: My Autobiography* (London: Hodder and Stoughton, 2000)

Heseltine, M., *No Stone Unturned: In Pursuit of Growth* (London: Department for Business Innovation and Skills, 2012)

Hinchliffe J., *Maritime Mercantile City* (Liverpool: Liverpool City Council, 2003)

Howell Williams, P., *Liverpolitania* (Liverpool: Merseyside Civic Society, 1971)

Hyland, P., *The Herculaneum Pottery* (Liverpool, 2006)

Joy, D. *Liverpool Cowkeepers* (Amberley Publishing, 2016)

Lancaster, B. H., *Liverpool and Her Potters* (Liverpool, 1936)

Lane, T., *City of The Sea* (Liverpool: Liverpool University Press, 1997)

Littlefield, D., *Liverpool One – Remaking A City Centre* (London: Wiley, 2009)

Liverpool City Council, *Liverpool Local Development Scheme: 2006* (Liverpool: Liverpool City Council, 2009)

Merseyside Socialist Research Group, *Merseyside In Crisis* (Birkenhead: Merseyside Socialist Group, 1980)

Macilwee, Michael, *The Liverpool Underworld* (Liverpool University Press, 2011)

Muir, R., *A History of Liverpool* (London: Published for The University Press of Liverpool By Williams and Norgate, 1907)

Murden, J., *City of Change and Challenge: Liverpool Since 1945* In J. Belchem
Paget-Tomlinson, E., *Illustrated History of Canal and River Navigation* (Sheffield, 1993)
Parkinson, M., *Liverpool on the Brink* (Oxford: Policy Journals, 1985)
Power, M., (Ed.), *Liverpool Town Books 1649-1671* (Stroud: Sutton Publishing Ltd, 1999)
Pye, K., *Liverpool: The Rise, Fall and Renaissance of a World Class City* (Amberley, 2014)
Stonehouse, James, *Recollections of Old Liverpool – By a Nonagerian: Liverpool: 1863* (F J Hughes, 1863)
Stonehouse, James, *The Streets of Liverpool: 1869* (Liverpool, 2002)
Thomas, H., *The Slave Trade: History of The Atlantic Slave Trade, 1440–1870* (New York: Simon and Schuster, 1997)
Various Contributors, *A Guide to Liverpool 1902* (London: Ward, Lock & Co., 1902)
Various Contributors, *Hamlyn's Menagerie Magazine* (London between 1915 and 1920)

## Websites

| | |
|---|---|
| Regia Anglorum | https://regia.org |
| Neston Town Council | https://www.neston.org.uk/ |
| Merseyside Mounted Police | https://merseysidepolicemounted.uk |
| Equine Heritage Institute | www.equineheritagemuseum.com |
| Looking at History Blog | http://richardjohnbr.blogspot.com/2008/04/horse-drawn-society.html |
| National Museums Liverpool | https://www.liverpoolmuseums.org.uk/stories/may-day-parades-proud-liverpool-tradition |
| Bank of England Inflation Calculator | www.bankofengland.co.uk/monetary-policy/inflation/inflation-calculator |

## Other Sources

Nicholas Blundell 's Diaries 1702–28 (Record Society of Lancashire and Cheshire)
Gore 's General Advertiser 1789 (Liverpool Record Office)
Williamson's Advertiser 1757 (Liverpool Record Office)

# Acknowledgements

There are several individuals and organisations who assisted my research, and who supported me during the writing of this book. In particular I would like to thank my many friends for their knowledge and encouragement, but especially my children, Ben, Sammy, and Danny, and my wife, Jackie.

For the sources for my stories, I would also like to acknowledge, as always, the professionalism and support of my fellow members of the Liverpool, Wavertree, Woolton, West Derby, Garston, and Gateacre Historical Societies; the librarians of The Athenaeum; and the staff of the Liverpool City Records Office.

Ken Pye
Liverpool 2022

# About the Author

Born and bred in Liverpool, Ken Pye was the Managing Director of The Knowledge Group in 2016. In a varied career spanning over fifty years, Ken has experience in each professional sector. This includes working as a Residential Child Care Officer for youngsters with profound special needs, as a Youth and Community Leader, as the Community Development Worker for Toxteth, as the Northwest Regional Officer for Barnardos, as the National Partnership Director for the Business Environment Association, and as Senior Programme Director with Common Purpose. He also undertook a special one-year contract for Liverpool Hope University as Executive Director of Continuing Professional Development, before setting up The Knowledge Group in 2009.

Ken is a Proprietor of the Athenaeum, and a Fellow of Liverpool Hope University.

Ken also continues as the Managing Director of his own local history company, Discover Liverpool, which he established in 2005. As such, he is a recognised expert on the past, present, and future potential of his home city and region. Ken is also a frequent contributor to journals, magazines, and newspapers. He is in great demand as and after-dinner speaker and guest lecturer to a wide range of groups and organisations, and is a regular broadcaster for both radio and television.

Well known across Merseyside and the North West as an expert in his field, Ken is the author of many books:

*Discover Liverpool* (now in its 3rd edition)
*A Brighter Hope* - about the founding and history of Liverpool Hope University
*Merseyside Tales* and *More Merseyside Tales*
*Liverpool: The Rise, Fall and Renaissance of a World Class City* – his complete history of the city, also in its 3rd edition
*Liverpool Pubs*
*The Bloody History of Liverpool* (now in its 3rd edition)
*Liverpool At Work*
*The A to Z of Little-Known Liverpool*
*Liverpool's Military Heritage*
*Two Triangles: Liverpool, Slavery, and The Church*
*Liverpool Murders and Misdemeanours*
*Even More Merseyside Tales*
*Liverpool: A Potted History*

Ken was also a significant contributor to Trinity Mirror's celebration of Liverpool and its people – *Scousers* – and the special advisor on *Sung and Unsung* – a collection of portrait photographs and biographies of the 'Great and the Good' of Liverpool.

Having also completed two books privately commissioned by the 19th Earl of Derby, Ken has also issued his set of four audio CDs on which he reads selections from his *Curious Characters and Tales of Merseyside*. Ken also produced three editions of his eight-volume filmed DVD documentary series *Discover Liverpool*.

On a personal basis and if pressed (better still, if taken out to dinner), Ken will regale you with tales from his own fascinating life, including his experiences during the Toxteth Riots, as a child entrepreneur, as a bingo caller, as a puppeteer, as the lead singer of a 1960s pop group, as an artists' and photographers' model, and as a mortuary attendant.

Ken is married to Jackie, and they have three grown-up children: Ben, Samantha, and Danny.

Visit Ken's website at www.discover-liverpool.com

Ken Pye with his family. (Discover Liverpool Library)